TRAVELERS

in search of

VACANCY

KAREN CLARK RASBERRY

ISBN: 978-0-615-32129-5 (Paperback)

Book design by Erin Rasberry Napier
Contribution by Phyllis Clark Holder
Author photograph by McAlister Creative

Printed in the United States of America

To my husband and children —
if not for them my life would contain many blank pages.

And to my parents —
whose memory tiptoes across my heart daily.

CONTENTS

Part 1:

NOWHERE

but here

WHY CAN'T I GET OVER ELVIS?

The other morning while I was getting dressed for work, Brian Kilmeade of Fox and Friends said the five-letter word that always stops me dead in my tracks. If what happened on August 16, 1977 is not indelibly etched into your memory, you probably will not care for this column. If you do know what happened on that sorrow-filled day three decades ago, you may have asked yourself a similar question. "Why can't I get over Elvis?"

Fox interviewed three of Elvis' best friends and highlighted a modernized replica of the 1957 Cadillac that he once owned. The Hershey Chocolate Company has produced a collector's edition of Reese's filled with peanut butter and banana cream, Elvis' favorite food combination, plus a chance to win the car. If this 30th anniversary of Elvis' demise has prompted such reaction from Hershey, I am relieved to know there is someone much higher up on the socioeconomic ladder that shares my same plight.

Many of my columns are written in my head while most normal people are sleeping. Last night was no different as I tried to pinpoint exactly why he still permeates my life thirty years A.D. For instance, why did my daughter's twenty-three year old boyfriend call me unexpectedly and sing "American Trilogy" to me at the top of his lungs while driving down the road? What would cause my son to belt out that same song as if he were Elvis re-incarnated? When the Ole Miss band plays their rousing version of "Dixie" to fire up the Rebels at football games, why do I only hear Elvis singing the words as he performed it in a 1976 concert at the Mississippi Coliseum?

Here are some disturbing facts that might need to be ana-lyzed. The most precious Christmas decoration I own is a miniature replica of Graceland all aglow complete with a pink Cadillac and tiny blinking trees. It is the lighting of Graceland, not the Christmas tree that officially launches the holiday season at my house. Furthermore, it is requisite that "Blue Christmas" be playing in the background when the lights come on in Elvis' house. Newspaper clippings from the day Elvis died are stored in the same safe place as my marriage license, birth certificate, and social security card. I've visited his grave four times and still hold out fading hope that it is empty. If *Blue Hawaii* aired on TV, I would watch every second of it even if Ringo Starr and Paul McCartney were performing together across the street at that precise moment.

In the wee hours of the morning, the answer finally came to me. It really isn't that complicated after all. Elvis and many of the people I've cherished were right there with me for some very important firsts and lasts in my life.

The first and last time I saw my daddy dance, he was teaching me to do the twist to "Jailhouse Rock." He threw his back out and never danced again. My sisters let me tag along with them like a big girl to see *Blue Hawaii* at the Arabian Theater. For the first time, I became very aware that there was an opposite sex, and for the rest of my life I would be attracted to it.

As an impressionable teenager, I saw Graceland for the first time with my very best friend. She moved away a few months later, and I never saw her again. It was Christmas, and Elvis was still very much alive and residing there. "Blue Christmas" was playing on the radio as we cruised past the front gates in the glow of the blue lights that decorated his lawn.

My first real date was to the South Mississippi Fair. "Burning Love" was blaring in the distance while I smooched with my first and only husband on the Ferris wheel. It wasn't my very first kiss, but it was the first and last time I was ever kissed on a Ferris wheel. A heart doesn't forget something like that.

While I was pregnant with my first child in 1976, I attended Elvis' last Mississippi concert in Jackson. He doesn't remember it, but my son danced for the first time. There had been a few thumps and bumps in my tummy, but Elvis' music literally made him dance with rhythm inside me. A mother never forgets that feeling of life inside her. The first songs my children learned were "Jesus Loves Me" and "Teddy Bear"—in that order.

My first and last encounter with E.S.P. happened on August 16, 1977. The day had an uneasy feel to it. I was rocking my six-month old son and watching TV when a special news alert flashed across the screen. "Memphis police report"—my heart stopped because I knew what they were about to say—"Elvis Presley died today at his Memphis mansion. He was forty-two years old." My sisters called me sobbing. From that day forward, all four of us have had a void in our lives that has never been filled by another singer.

Thankfully, the music didn't die that day, and Elvis continues to provide the soundtrack to my life. In my old age, I hope "Jailhouse Rock" will inspire me to rise from my wheelchair and swivel my hips, and that "Burning Love" will always give me that same weightless, forever young feeling as kissing on a Ferris wheel.

A LITTLE PIECE OF HEAVEN

The Magnolia State and Jones County have always been my home. It is where I was born, and in all probability, it is where I will die. My paternal great-grandparents, George Washington Clark and Mattie Green Clark, staked out a little piece of ground in the piney woods of northeast Jones County in the late 1800's. My maternal ancestral roots run even deeper and wider in this county. The branches of that family tree include such surnames as Williams, Black and Knight. I can "rake up" kin with practically every resident in this county.

If family trees could be identified by species, I would want mine to be the *Magnolia Grandiflora*—our state tree.

When traveling up north, I love saying I'm from Mississippi. I have very few good memories that did not come from within its boundaries. Once, I visited Minneapolis, Minnesota, for a week in

August. The mosquitoes were as big as hummingbirds and would eat you alive if you didn't keep moving. Most of the women there had skin the color of bleu cheese dressing and said "yah" and "ah" a lot. They had the gall to make fun of my accent.

San Francisco is one of the most beautiful places I have ever visited, but it is inhabited by very bizarre, unsociable people. Just one person out of the thousands I naively smiled at tried to make conversation. When I explained that my accent was Mississippian, not Texan, she disgustedly looked down at my feet and was surprised to see I was wearing shoes. Mark Twain said, and I agree 100%, "the coldest winter I ever spent was June in San Francisco."

Everyone should visit New York City at least once because it truly is a living monument to the commercialism of mankind. When you hail from such an idyllic town as Laurel, you will leave there with a deep appreciation for slow-talking, small-town life. My husband refuses to make the trip because of this line in a Hank Williams, Jr. song, "Just send me to hell or New York City. It would be about the same to me."

Obviously, much of the mystique that surrounds our state comes from the mighty, muddy river that marks our boundary to the west. Mississippi also has miles of beautiful coastline and lush, rolling pine forests. When that coastline was utterly destroyed by Hurricane Katrina, those Mississippians didn't stand around pointing fingers and blaming others for nature's wrath. They picked through the ruins and resolved to rebuild because of their love for this unique state and our extraordinary way of life.

How I love Natchez, where the traditions and gentility of

the Old South are still the main attraction for thousands of pilgrims from every corner of the world. Then, you must consider our very cosmopolitan capital city of Jackson—rich in history, entertainment venues, museums and galleries.

Mississippi also has hundreds of sleepy little crossroad towns such as Hot Coffee, Soso, and Sandersville, where folks talk and move about at a slower pace, openly praise the Lord on Sunday mornings, and are generally made of the good, strong glue that holds a society together.

The most amazing thing about this state is its contribution to the arts and entertainment world. It's hard to conceive how others can cast stones at the state that rocked the cradle of opera legend Leontyne Price and put the swivel in the hips of Elvis Presley.

No other state can claim a richer per capita contribution of literary and entertainment genius. William Faulkner, Willie Morris, Eudora Welty, Tennessee Williams and John Grisham are all Mississippians—as are Tammy Wynette, Faith Hill, Conway Twitty, Jimmy Rogers, Oprah Winfrey, Jimmy Buffett, Morgan Freeman and James Earl Jones.

World-class athletes. We all have our favorites, raised up from Mississippi soil, who represent our chosen sports teams and alma maters. There's not enough space in this medium to adequately praise them all.

Much of our nation's monumental medical progress has roots in Mississippi. The first heart transplant in 1964. The first lung transplant in 1963. We test space shuttle engines for NASA and build ships that help defend our freedom. The Nissan plant just outside of Canton has the staggering capacity to manufacture 400,000 automobiles per year. The list goes on and on.

Perhaps, Mississippi shouldn't tempt others by flaunting its opportunities, wonderful climate and southern hospitality. The truth is we are a poor state rich in natural and human resources, and we must market our attributes to the world in order to scratch our way out of the bottom of the heap. It is my fear that eventually everyone will know what we have known all along. There's a little piece of Heaven just east of the mighty Mississippi and due south of the Mason-Dixon Line.

Ya'll come on down now and visit a spell. Dip your toes in the Gulf of Mexico. Have a glass of sweet iced tea. Marvel at how friendly the people are. Just don't wear your welcome out.

BEING SCARLETT O'HARA

I love being a native Mississippian and relish the reaction that people in unenlightened places have when they realize where I'm from. I suppose they are just a bit disappointed to see a real live Mississippian who doesn't adhere to their stereotype of being barefoot, backwards and bigoted. A few years ago, I visited San Francisco with my daughter and daughter-in-law. On one occasion, I was wearing a t-shirt emblazoned with an emblem that revealed my Mississippi roots when I started craving a snack. A snobbish clerk in the hotel sundry shop leaned over the counter and peered down at my feet after I slowly and sweetly asked if she had a "pack o' nabs and a Coke." I suppose she wanted to see if I had on any shoes.

We are all kindred spirits who never completely pull our roots out of the rich Mississippi earth—no matter where we might find ourselves living and growing. After some time spent soul searching, I believe that it truly is the land which nourishes our character, strength and identity. It's no secret that talent seems to proliferate among those who have gotten some Mississippi mud between their toes.

I quietly pondered all of this on the way back from a wedding in Natchez last weekend. Mention Natchez, and the mind conjures up columns, azaleas, mansions and magnolias. Although Natchez sits precariously atop the bluffs of the river that gave it life, the city clings tightly to its antebellum past. It's not that we Mississippians want to resurrect the past, we just don't want to bury our unique heritage without a tombstone and pretend it never happened.

Through the hospitality of a friend of a friend, we were guests for the weekend at an authentic antebellum cottage. The cottage was built by a wealthy planter for his African overseer around 1850 and is listed on the National Register of Historic Places. The same African became a free man of color and bought the home at auction after the war left the planter in financial ruin. The history and antiquity of the surrounding land and home saddened and thrilled me at the same time. If its walls could talk and the land could tell stories of the blood, sweat and toil, what an epic tale it would be. It is far off the beaten path, and information about it is not included on any tourist brochures. In fact, I am hesitant to mention it in this column because of the owner's intentional wish for obscurity. You must ford a creek by way of an SUV or truck to access this antebellum treasure. If it comes a rainstorm, guests can become stranded in the mid 19th Century—not a bad plight in my opinion. When the rain started pouring on Sunday morning, it gave new meaning to the old adage, "If the creek don't rise." An ancient twisted oak that has obviously weathered the storms of war and more than a few hurricanes stands watch over the front porch. The perfect scene of the antebellum South made me want to run with a hoop skirt pulled above my knees into the arms of Captain Rhett Butler.

The outdoor wedding was held on the steps of Rosalie (circa 1820), which is situated on a bluff overlooking the Mississippi River. It was the fairy tale wedding the bride had always dreamed of. Her billowy satin gown harkened back to the days of hoop skirts, soirees and mint juleps. The scent of magnolia blossoms, muddy water and rose petals filled the air. Except for the imposing sound of tour buses straining to rise from Natchez Under the Hill, the year could just as well have been 1861. Once again, I fancied myself as Scarlett at the fateful Twelve Oaks picnic on the eve of the Civil War.

Later that night after the wedding, we made our way across the creek to the cottage. For the first time in my life I slept in a canopied bed inside an antebellum home. I awakened trying to remember these words from *Gone With the Wind* that echoed in and out of my weekend of being Scarlett O'Hara.

"Do you mean to tell me Katie Scarlett O'Hara, that Tara, that land doesn't mean anything to you? Why, land is the only thing in the world worth workin' for, worth fightin' for, worth dyin' for, because it's the only thing that lasts. It will come to you, this love of land."

Gerald O'Hara was right. It's the love of the land and this place called Mississippi that eventually gets inside your soul. Just as it was in 1861, and as it is unto this day.

PUTTIN' ON THE SQUEEZE

We Southerners hug. It's reassuring to know that while the rest of the world worries itself with less meaningful greetings, we are quite comfortable with the big squeeze.

Everybody hugs everybody in the South. Uncles bear-hug nephews and then challenge them to an arm wrestling match. Mothers hug their children with a warm pat on the back and an extra mmm-mmm-mmm, which is mom-speak for "you are precious, and I love you." Dads toss toddlers into the air and swoop them into hugs on their descent back to Earth. Bubbly cheerleaders spring onto tiptoes for a hug from football heroes. Manly coaches hug burly linebackers. Smiling beauty pageant losers hug the winner even though they'd kill to be the one wearing that coveted crown. Grandmas smother grandchildren in the feather bed of their ample bosoms. When I'd have rather shattered my tennis racquet into a million pieces after being totally humiliated in a match, I've even hugged my opponents across the net. Happy new homeowners often hug realtors at closing when the day before they threatened a lawsuit over such issues as possession of a wagon wheel chandelier or dead powder post beetles. Total strangers hug upon realizing that they have just met their sister's college roommate's mother's best friend from Savannah. Out of respect for tradition and a legendary rivalry, even Ole Miss and Mississippi State alums will give the old passing, "hotty toddy," "go dawgs," one-arm hug. I've decided that hugging, in addition to being a display of warmth and affection, is often an action performed by graceful winners and losers.

As I was writing this, I asked my husband, our resident Civil War expert, if he thought that the Southern gentleman Robert E. Lee hugged General Grant's neck after he surrendered to him at Appomattox. "Not a snowball's chance in Hell," he answered solemnly. He then enlightened me to the fact that there are limits to Southern gentility.

No one can deny that we are a friendly bunch of folks, yet there is a growing threat to the hug. Southerners living in certain parts of the country have adopted the foreign ways of Californians and the French. They kiss hello in public. Yes, kiss. Sometimes it's one ever so slight peck on the cheek, or it might be a perfunctory kiss on both. And, worst of all, sometimes there could be another smack into the perfumed air around the cheek. The kiss can confuse well-meaning Southerners going in for a hug. A kiss-hug collision may result, with the kisser more likely to be offended by the over-familiarity of the hugger. Therefore, it is imperative that Southerners not confuse cheek kissing with actual affection. If you are in Paris do as the Parisians do. When you are in the South, quit putting on airs, and hug.

Handshakes, too, present problems. To shake or not to shake, that is the question. Done poorly or not at all at a job interview or when meeting someone for the first time, it can make or break a first impression. Too weak might indicate a lack of character. Too strong might be a sign of insecurity. Too enthusiastic reeks of desperation. Too brief conveys laziness. Then there's limp, clammy, sweaty, dead-fishy, wonder where it's been, and, let's not forget, the perennial bone-crushing handshake.

On Sunday mornings at Bethlehem Baptist Church, we have a meet and greet session as a prelude to worship. My most memorable handshakes of all time came from a precious gentleman whom I nicknamed "The Crusher." He would invariably latch on to my right hand and proceed to squeeze and pump my hand and fingers, much like he was milking a cow, while talking to my husband about this and that for what seemed to be the length of a longwinded sermon. On several occasions, he all but squeezed blood from my fingers and often brought tears to my eyes. After several years, I learned to keep an eye out for him and would preemptively slip only my fingertips into his massive hand. Now that he has passed away, I would gladly endure a little pain to once again see that undeniable light of Christian love in his face. Even so, handshakes seem to be going the way of the necktie, a contrivance saved for job interviews, weddings and funerals.

I am thankful that the good old-fashioned, heart-to-heart hug, still reigns supreme here in the South. When it comes time to greet an old friend, to welcome a soldier home, to divide grief, to multiply joy, to comfort a hurting child, to reassure the elderly, or simply to say, "I care," nothing does it better than the humble hug.

Part 2:

ROOTS

and wings

THE LOST ART OF PORCH SITTING

One hot afternoon while sweeping, attempting CPR on my gravely ill geraniums and battling wasps on my front porch, it crossed my mind that life would be so much easier if my house had been built porchless. I can count on one hand how many times anyone has earnestly sat on it during the past fifteen years. My son and his wife did sit on it cuddled up under a quilt a few times when they came home from Florida for the holidays. It was where they tried to soak up enough home to tide them over until their next visit. Since they moved back to Jones County over a year ago, only wasps and lizards enjoy my front porch.

My childhood home had a screened front porch. Both of my grandparents had houses with front porches. Consequently, I practiced more than my share of the lost art of porch sitting on all three of them during my childhood. A child can learn a whole lot while sitting on a front porch.

My maternal grandmother, Helen Fairbell Williams Black, was the most revered of the porch sitters in our community. One of the things that I learned while sitting on her porch was that I hate shelling peas. Accompanied by her squeaky porch swing, she would sit there for hours singing and humming her favorite gospel hymns. She would hum "The Old Rugged Cross" as her arthritic fingers worked. Her eyes were failing and her glasses were in desperate need of a cleaning, so I served as her watchdog. As cars whizzed by in a red cloud of dust, she would always ask me who it was. When I answered, she would speculate about the destination of every passerby. "Oh, it's Saturday, I bet that "so and so" is going to Laurel to buy some whiskey." Then she would put me on alert. "If you hear the preacher's car coming down the hill, run out to the mailbox and flag him down. I want to give him a mess of peas and tell him he needs to pray for 'so and so.'" And then she would wish out loud, "I sure do hope the Rawley Man brings me my liniment. All this pea shelling has made my fingers stiff as pokers." To complain about pea shelling would have been disrespectful to her and everything that is good and true in the world. While sitting on her front porch, I learned to respect my elders.

While pondering the absence of sittable porches due to the

architecture of new homes and the lack of porch sitters at homes like mine, guilt washed over me for wishing that my front porch didn't exist. We are now in grave danger of losing that relaxed, down-home way of life that has been synonymous with the South since Mason and Dixon drew that line.

The demise of porch sitting is attributable mainly to three things: air-conditioning, television, and the fact that we have become too busy and important for our own good. We have worked around the clock to accumulate so many tangible things that we no longer have the time to enjoy the little things that a paycheck can't buy.

Porch sitting wasn't without its perils. My grandparents had an attack rooster that was prone to run up the steps and spur unsuspecting porch sitters. That tough old bird wound up in a pot of dumplings. While sitting in a chair that was precariously close to the porch's edge, my grandfather once spat tobacco juice so vigorously that he pitched head first, four feet to the ground. Nobody could figure why it didn't kill him. For most of his remaining days, he sat contentedly (albeit a little further back from the edge) on his front porch watching the world go by. While trying to give away a mess of peas, my grandmother fell on the porch and broke her hip after her feet got tangled up with a stray tomcat.

As I was sitting out on my front porch last night in an attempt to assuage my guilt, a magnificent theory came to me. Maybe, just maybe, instead of mansions sitting on streets of gold, Heaven offers creaky old houses with wide front porches that sit alongside endless dirt roads as an alternative for the porch sitters who never coveted anything on this earth. My theory is probably not true; but if it is, I am certain that my grandparents, recently joined by my parents, are all together shelling, singing, spitting (if it is allowed) and watching to see who is coming up the road next.

THE MAN WITH MAGICAL HANDS

My paternal grandfather, Herman G. Clark, was in the neck and back business. On certain days that are becoming too frequent, when my sciatica acts up or I can't turn my head to back up my car, I long to hop on my bicycle and take a short ride to his house for a "treatment." In 1915, at the age of 20, he received his chiropractor's diploma through a mail-order program from the National School of Chiropractic in Chicago, Illinois. Unlike my husband, who practices the kindred profession of physical therapy, he never doubted that my woes were genuine and in need of immediate attention by his loving hands.

Other than his ten surviving grandchildren and one daughter, few people remain who can attest to obtaining relief from his magical hands. A few months ago, while waiting at the doctor's office with my mother-in-law, a congenial gentleman who was up in his years struck up a conversation with me out of abject boredom. It proved to be just one more thing I love about being from the South. You can strike up a conversation with a perfect stranger, and within two minutes you've raked up kin upon discovering that his mother was a first cousin once removed to your beloved grandmother or that his son graduated high school with and had a crush on your sister in 1965. This vaguely familiar character from the suburbs of Eucutta (pronounced "you cutty" by the natives) clearly remembered my father and my grandfather and had found relief on his treatment table numerous times. Oblivious to the urgency and sickness around us, we talked and reminisced through the flow of the fevered and infirm until my mother-in-law emerged from a testing room. I didn't know whether to hug him, ask him and his wife over for a barbecue or simply thank him for reinforcing my long-held faith in my grandfather's magical hands and that I had not been suffering from prejudiced, granddaughterly illusions for the majority of my life. Although we said our goodbyes without hugging or fanfare, I felt a little sad leaving the company of a man who had actually been touched by the man I loved so much.

I often wonder what my grandfather would have to say about modern technology and the state of the world today. He was born in a log house five miles east of Sandersville in 1895. Practically every day of his life was spent on the same piece of ground that his parents homesteaded shortly after the Civil War. In the beginning years of his practice, he made house calls in a horse and buggy when word came that a neighbor was flat on his back and in need of an "adjustment." After World War I, he made his rounds in a Model-A Ford—the same car that my daddy learned to drive when he was knee high to a grasshopper and barely able to see over the steering wheel. In later years he built an office adjoining his house. Since no appointment was required, patients from near and far showed up at all hours of the day and night. The afflicted often entered with a visible hitch in their "get along" and a pained look on their faces but exited a few minutes later with a smile and a spring in their step

His life was long and blessed allowing him to witness many astonishing events. His heart went with them when he sent his two sons to fight in the second Great War. His joy and gratefulness were immeasurable when they both returned unharmed. With terrorist activity and the atrocities of 9-11 being comparable to Hitler's attempts at killing his sons, I'm positive he wouldn't be opposed to a little water boarding to insure that your sons and daughters stay alive. In his lifetime, he marveled over the feats of both the Wright brothers and John Glenn. Since he traded in a brown mule for a red Mustang in 1969, I'm certain that he would be saddened by the state of the American auto industry. He was appalled when the rebellious '60s rolled around and couldn't abide how short we granddaughters wore our skirts. Even though he was a man ahead of his times, I shudder to think what he would have thought about same-sex marriage, gender switching and the overall moral decay of our nation.

Tonight, as I sit here writing with a crick in my neck, an ache in my back and little hope of sympathy from my husband, my maladies are quietly soothed by the distinct smell of pipe tobacco, the sensation of being lowered into a prone position on his treatment table, and the remembrance of my grandfather's magical healing hands.

REMEMBER TO THANK A VETERAN

In the almost four years that he has been gone, like last Saturday, in the slanting light of a perfect fall day, he comes to me at the least expected times. I was puttering in my yard when a squirrel scampered from our Katrina-ravaged pecan tree and disappeared into the woods. I thought I heard his voice, "Look! Baby, there's a squirrel. Brace the gun on your shoulder, and aim a little ahead of him."

My daddy, Ralph Gayle Clark, was a man who didn't have the luxury of sons to take hunting or to watch with pride as they played sports. He had no eager man-child that he could show the proper way to wash a car, handle a gun, scale a fish, or drive a stick shift. There were no offspring on the brink of manhood that he could stand toe to toe with, look into his eyes and know that his surname would at least reach into the next generation. He and my mother gave it one last try, but the fourth attempt produced the same results. Another girl. Me. His baby. It's not that he loved me more than the other three girls, it's that I came along later in his life, a grand finale of sorts, his last chance at immortality. Instead of longing for what he would never have, he resolved to make the most of the hand that he had been dealt.

He faithfully attended every football game at old Sandersville High School to watch my sisters twirl their batons and to root for his friends' sons. One by one, he reluctantly became the father of three brides. Letting go became easier each time as he learned that you can't stop love or fence time and that daughters will love their daddies even if they carry another man's last name.

So, there I was, a solitary girl child, left behind by her older sisters. My father and I became hunting, fishing and shopping buddies. He taught me how to shake a squirrel out of its nest by pulling vines and how to aim at a moving target with a shotgun. When I entered high school, he attended every home game and watched me cheer out of the corner of one eye and the game with the other. He took me shopping for bell-bottomed jeans and go-go boots. We liked to cruise through new car lots and talk about horsepower. In 1969, he must have finally made his peace with the Empire of Japan for trying to kill him at Pearl Harbor when he purchased an aqua-blue, five-speed Datsun pickup truck. I always wanted a Volkswagen Beetle, but he just couldn't get right with the Germans for lobbing large shells toward his tiny minesweeper on D-Day. However, he figured the Japanese paid for their transgressions one-hundred fold at Hiroshima, thus justifying his purchase, "If they build trucks like they fought in World War II, this ought to be one heckuva mosheen."

Patience was not his best virtue, but he rose to the challenge and eventually taught me how to shift gears in his new import without giving him whiplash. It's been almost four decades, but I still hear him through the ears of a fourteen-year old girl, "Easy now sugar, let off the clutch and give it a little gas at the same time. (jerk) No! (screech) Nooo! I said eeeeasy, doll baby, not like a jack rabbit."

When his health was failing, and we girls took turns chauffeuring him to doctor visits, one day his voice quivered when he said, "Sugar, you know how to maneuver a car just right and can do anything a man can do. It was real great that I had four girls." That is the finest compliment I ever received from anyone. He was often troubled and spent much of his life wrestling with the demons that accompanied him home from WWII. The war was something he rarely talked about in the first person, and we knew better than to ask.

After watching the premier of Ken Burn's highly acclaimed documentary, *The War*, I learned that not talking about the war was the norm for that generation of returning soldiers. Though in the last episode, many of them finally opened up and shared memories that had been buried deep inside them for sixty years. Nothing presented in any media has ever brought as many tears and affected me so profoundly. For some reason, my heart hurt as if I had lost my daddy all over again. All those old soldiers took on his persona. Their voices became his voice. Their stories were his stories--the ones he rationed out in bits and pieces.

The once youthful heroes who saved the world from tyranny are dying at the rate of 1,000 per day. In a few short years, all of them will be gone. Those that remain, as well as all veterans from every war, must be thanked now before it's too late. In the most gracious way I know how, I humbly offer my thanks.

A JOURNEY TO UNDERSTANDING FREEDOM

The first time I visited Washington, D.C., it was the summer of 1966. A tall, slow-talking Texan, L.B.J., was in the White House. The Vietnam conflict was escalating into a full-fledged war, and we were completely unaware that we were poised on the edge of a social volcano that would erupt over the next several years.

The second time was thirty-one years later in 1997 when my husband and I served as chaperones to a tour bus full of hyperactive 6th and 7th graders. It was on that return trip to the nation's Capitol as an adult, that I finally realized why my father made his pilgrimage all those years ago.

When our bus mercifully rolled into Washington, it was surprising how my memory had failed me. I didn't remember the city as being beautiful—just busy and confusing with a maze of one-way streets that had kept my daddy in constant fear of making another wrong turn. The monuments were still there, even larger with the passing of time, standing vigil over the great halls of freedom and justice. A rush of patriotism swept over me, and the odd feeling that the spirits of those who had foreordained my freedom were still there.

On the second day of whirlwind touring, we finally made our way across the Potomac into Arlington, where our students would participate in a wreath-laying ceremony at the Tomb of the Unknowns. For as far as the eye could see, simple white markers stood in perfect military formation—each one representing a life unselfishly laid down in the name of freedom.

The monument is inscribed with the words, "Here rests in honored glory an American soldier known but to God." Sentinels guard it day and night with a display of military precision and symbolism that filled me with so much pride that I couldn't hold back my tears. I was shaken right down to my soul, deeply grateful and even ashamed that I had never made any personal sacrifice for my own freedom. And, I wondered if I would have the courage to gracefully give up a son, daughter, husband or father if freedom demanded it. Naturally, I thought about the humble World War II veteran who took me there in 1966. I began to understand.

Not until he had stood at the tomb with his hat over his heart could he move on and accept that so many comrades in arms had fallen in order to make better lives for those who survived. I suddenly had a vision of my daddy removing his glasses as he pulled a handkerchief from his back pocket.

On our last day in Washington, we visited the black granite wall that is the Vietnam War Memorial. It was my mission to find two names on the wall. In 1970, at a Naval air show in Meridian, I paid $5.00 for a POW-MIA bracelet. I proudly wore it for two years, never taking it off for one second, until one day it broke in half. Brokenhearted, I placed the pieces in a dresser drawer, eventually forgetting the soldier's name but not the reasons I wore it so faithfully. When I approached the wall, the name of the soldier came to me in a revelation—Lt. Steven R. Armitstead. Just as I had feared, he was listed among those known killed in the Vietnam War. I carefully made a pencil etching of his name along with an etching of the name of my second cousin, Elmer D. Hill, of Sharon. My mind flashed back to his funeral—a mother's tears, a folded flag, and the mournful sound of a lone bugler playing "Taps."

We pulled out of Washington that night—tired, wet and chilled to the bone from April showers. On the long trip back home to Mississippi, I couldn't stop thinking about Steven R. Armitstead, Elmer D. Hill, and all the countless others who paid for my freedom in places like Bataan, Pearl Harbor, Omaha Beach, Khe Sanh and a thousand other ungodly battlefields.

If my daddy were here today, I would thank him for that trip in the summer of 1966. Now, I know that it was a journey to understanding what he and his generation had done for my sisters and me even before we were born. I would hug him and tell him he is my hero. I would tell him that I will never forget his service to this country and that an American flag will always fly from my front porch on patriotic holidays. I would tell him that it is an honor to be his daughter.

CONFESSIONS OF A WAR BRIDE

Hardly a day passes that she doesn't tip toe across my consciousness.
It's impossible not to think about my mother when there are reminders everywhere I turn in my house. She lives on in an antique teapot that has occupied my kitchen window for over fifteen years. With her green thumb, she took a pinky finger-sized sprig of cactus and potted it in leafy soil she had collected from the edge of the woods in her back yard. She insisted that I take it home even though she figured its days were numbered. Today, with no special care from me, it is over a foot tall and has hundreds of prickly fingers that reach

toward the morning sun. I water it haphazardly and never actually remember the last time I did. It outgrew the teapot years ago, but I'm certain that if I try to repot it, my brown thumb will cause it to wither away. I want it to live forever so I leave it be.

On certain days, I find myself staring at the gallery of family photos I have clustered on a wall near my back door. Among the pictures is my very favorite one of my parents when they were newly wed and just beginning their sixty-two year journey into married life. It is impossible for me to look at that photo and not smile.

Taken in April of 1942, a few days after they married, they are as forever entwined as the wisteria on the picket fence in the background. Fresh off the U.S.S. Indianapolis and still reeling from Pearl Harbor, my daddy looks rail-thin and tall in black pants and a Navy issue t-shirt. My mother, the exultant but reluctant bride, is dressed in a plaid, knee-length skirt and a white pin-up worthy sweater. She wears it well.

In 1938, at the age of nineteen, my daddy joined the Navy. Of course, the war didn't begin until 1941, but he was restless to see what was at the end of that red dirt road that ran past his house. Before he left, he walked a half-mile west down that road to where my mother lived. His intent was to tell her that he was going to marry her one day, but she was visiting a friend in town. The next day, before my grandfather delivered him to the train depot, my daddy persuaded him to stop by the house where my mother was visiting. Since she was only fifteen and ambivalent about her feelings toward him, she made him no promises. And so, he embarked on an adventure that changed his life and the world and accordingly set the course for all of us who came afterwards.

Four years later and now an inductee into the solemn mysteries of the ancient order of the deep, my father showed up tanned and gaunt at the downtown drugstore where my mother worked. He matter of factly informed her that she was going to be his wife. She didn't say yes or no, but found herself at the courthouse early the next morning applying for a marriage license. When my daddy set sail a week later, she had a new last name and a baby on the way.

My oldest sister was a war baby, and my mother always jokingly confessed that she was born nine months and one hour after the wedding. When I think about the hardships that she endured as a new mother during the war years, that is when I am the most grateful to her. She nursed my sister discreetly on military trains and spent weeks alone in port cities waiting for any word from her sailor. All the while she battled bedbugs, roaches, and incurable homesickness and prayed that her baby would not be fatherless when the war finally ended.

When I am standing in front of my stove, I have a perfect view of the portrait my daughter painted of that favorite picture. It is the way I like to think of her. It is 1942. She is a blushing bride of nineteen who still has sixty-two years to grow her love for the handsome sailor. She always did have a knack for growing things. With a Hollywood smile and white sweater that could have given Rita Hayworth a run for her money, she has no idea how beautiful she is or what the future holds. She was my mother.

A CONVERSATION WITH MY DADDY

All day long, on this the 67th anniversary of the bombing of Pearl Harbor, I could sense the presence of my daddy everywhere. I wanted desperately to talk to him and ask a few questions about that day, but he and the answers have been gone for nearly five years. I guess it's because yesterday was a rare day spent reminiscing with my children and old friends about Christmases past that made me keenly aware of those who are no longer here with me.

It seems that the infamous day that the Japanese bombed Pearl Harbor is commemorated less and less each year. Those young men and women who saved the world over sixty years ago were once courageous and invincible; and now they are becoming extinct.

When my daddy passed away, we found among his keepsakes, his continuous service certificate from his first enlistment in the Navy. It is a small, green quad-fold book embossed in gold with the Department of the Navy seal. It is in pristine condition, not ragged or worn as you might expect considering its age and the perilous miles at sea it traveled. For the past four years, whenever I feel like having a conversation with my daddy, I can sometimes find his voice in the book.

The first entry was typed on April 12, 1938, at the Navy recruiting station in New Orleans. The last entry was on April 7, 1943 in Beaumont, Texas. Many answers to many questions of the ancient order of the deep are written between the lines on the pages of this abbreviated journal that I now hold in my hands. Although the entries are impersonal, are typed with military brevity, and leave much to my imagination, it has become a biography of sorts for the man who speaks to me through it.

The conversation I wanted to have with my daddy Sunday morning was this: Do you think FDR suspected that the Japanese were going to attack Pearl Harbor and why was your ship out to sea? The answers lie not in what the little green book said, but in its very existence as proof that FDR did suspect an attack on Pearl Harbor and was preparing for the United States to enter the war.

Although the loss of life and five battleships was horrific and shocked the nation, history tends to ignore the fact that most of the Pacific fleet that could and should have been in harbor was not. In fact, the Pacific fleet did not have enough oil at Pearl Harbor to keep the ships at sea. Nevertheless, the *U.S.S. Indianapolis*, the flagship of the Pacific fleet, and five destroyer minesweepers were making a simulated bombardment of Johnston Island (700 NM W of Hawaii) on the morning of December 7, 1941. Herein lies the truth to the controversial question. FDR did know; and he was preparing for a sneak attack by the Japanese. They were just too darned sneaky and brazen to predict. The battleships were sent back to port because they were unable to keep up with the dozens of destroyers, submarines, carriers and cruisers that were preparing for war in the Pacific. The somber truth is that if the Indy had been a battleship, the little green book sitting in front of me most likely would have been destroyed, and I probably would not be here today.

My next topic of conversation with my daddy was this: What did the Indianapolis do once war was declared by the United States? With a little more online research and a rare, telling entry in the service book, I heard his answer as clearly as if it had come straight from his mouth:

Indianapolis, Feb. 6, 1942, QM2c Ralph Gayle Clark. Crossed equator. Qualified Shellback. Qualified as member of "Realm of the Golden Dragon" by crossing the 180th. Meridian. Member of Task Force Eleven Commended by Commander, Task Force Eleven for efficient support given air force and for outstanding engineering performance during two successful engagements against enemy attacks, period between 1-31-42 & 3-30-42, the result of which inflicted serious damage to enemy. Expiration of Enl. Honorable. Yes.

After serving four years in the Navy, the green book tells me my daddy re-enlisted at Pearl Harbor for four more years. He said his final farewell to the Indy at Mare Island in California then returned to Norfolk, Virginia on March 31, 1942. A couple of days later, he stepped off the train in Laurel, Mississippi. Still in uniform and with his bag slung over his shoulder, he found his land-legs again and hurried across the tracks to downtown. He entered Walgreen's where he found the courage to ask my mother to marry him. She said yes.

Daddy, I'm so glad we had this conversation. We'll talk again real soon.

THE BUTTON JAR

Several mornings ago as my husband was dressing for church, he couldn't button a cuff of his shirt because the dry cleaners had crushed the button. Hurriedly, I went to the closet to fetch my sewing box, a plastic, gold colored relic from my high school home economics class, to look for a replacement. The box flew open and all of its pitiful contents spilled across the floor.

What started out as one of those every day little mishaps of life became an urgent need to remember a woman who once had been, but is now no more. After an interval of months or longer, the memory of my grandmother came upon me.

Among her many other talents, Ola Sims Clark was a seamstress. In the pantry of her house along with her canned pickles, tomatoes and pepper sauce, was a jar of buttons, each one left over from her sewing or mending projects. After enduring the hardships of the Great Depression, discarding anything, much less a valuable button, would not have been an act of a virtuous woman.

Her pantry shelves were full of various and sundry items that were commonly found in every rural Southern household—garden seeds, mothballs, elixir bottles, and Prince Albert tobacco cans full of nails, tacks, screws and trinkets of mysterious origin and usage. As helplessly as the flies stuck to the flypaper hanging from the ceiling, I was captivated by the charms of her pantry.

If I squeeze my eyes tightly and manage to block out all the modern chaos that surrounds me, I am able to transcend time and place back to 1965. I am not here at my computer but standing in my grandmother's pantry. The washing machine is playing a familiar song as I open the door. Dirt daubers are buzzing and bumping the window screen outside. The room is stuffy and thick with the smells of detergent, mothballs and green onions. The fragrances are not like my favorite ones of cotton candy at the fair, popcorn at the Arabian Theatre and the nut stand in Sears, but it is not unpleasant here. The treasure that I seek is at my eye level, left there intentionally for me by my grandmother. If that Mason jar had been filled to overflowing with diamonds, sapphires and gold as I imagined they were, instead of colored glass, plastic and tarnished metal, it would have made no difference to her. In her world, buttons were more valuable than jewels.

We shared many quiet hours at her dining room table, which did double duty as a sewing table. Although her head shook from a benign palsy, her hands were steady and sure when she worked her magic with fabrics. With her serrated tracing wheel, it was my duty and pleasure to trace the pattern of my dresses onto the material. The bond that held us together was more enduring than the stitches she sewed with her Singer sewing machine.

In October of 1965, my grandmother gave me a purple jumper with a yellow blouse that she had sewn for my 10th birthday. Ten days later cancer claimed her life, and she physically left my world.

I must confess that after forty-two years, thoughts of her don't come often. When they do, they are mostly random and provoked by the simplest of things. I see her face only faintly now and pictures of her don't really match my mind's eye. Yet, the memory of her hugs is as vivid as ever. She visits me most often with the changing of the seasons, in flowers, and in blue October skies. When wisteria blooms lavender in Spring, I imagine her planting the first vine that eventually smothered the fence in front of her house. She taught me that crepe myrtles weep in July and that Magnolia blossoms are not intended for vases but best enjoyed on warm June breezes. The color purple still reminds me of that jumper.

Sunday morning was not the first time that I had thought about the button jar. Years ago I asked my aunt if she knew whatever happened to her mother's button collection. To my surprise, it had been in her possession all these years when I thought it was lost forever. When I first held them in my hands again, they seemed so ordinary and pilfered, not the jewels they were when I was ten. My aunt told me I could keep them since they meant so much to me. I told her I would like to keep my memories instead.

IT'S WATERMELON CUTTIN' TIME

The third name on my mother's roll call, Phyllis Holder, called me Saturday to see if I was still kicking. We don't talk as often as we should because both of us are so busy doing different things. She is at one phase in her life, and I am in another. She is in the middle of building a house, enjoying retirement and being a grandmother. I am, well, planning a wedding, care giving, trying to sell a little real estate, string a few words together and, according to my daughter, playing too much tennis. She wonders if I will be off the tennis circuit in time to attend her wedding in November.

All that aside, sis wanted to know why she didn't see my column in the Review last week. I explained that the heat had gotten to my brain, and I couldn't think of a thing to write for you discerning readers.

She suggested that I should write about how granddaddy used to cut a watermelon every afternoon in the summer when we were kids.

She was onto something with the watermelon story, but I told her I remembered so little about it—only the seed-spittin' wars and how somebody always put salt on theirs and how silly it seemed to put salt on something so perfectly sweet. Since she is the poet of the family, I suggested that she write her remembrances for me. Only a sister would do such a great favor.

The words that follow are a joint sister act that recalls watermelon cuttin' on Clark Hill.

Just five miles east of being on the map, down Eucutta Road, at the peak of Clark Hill—stands a little piece of Heaven on earth. I grew up there in the 50's and 60's with my three sisters—Charlotte, Marilyn and Karen—and a host of other blood relatives.

Heaven was so hot during those Mississippi summers that we couldn't coax our dog out from under the shade of the porch with a bone. The only air-conditioning we had was the kind that nature provided when the wind blew. However, our PaPa Clark had his own way of helping his grandchildren beat the heat in the summertime.

My paternal grandparents were Ola Sims Clark and Herman G. Clark. PaPa was born on Clark Hill in 1895 and spent the majority of his 86 years there. I only spent the first eighteen years of mine there in a white house with a front porch that had a great view of a dusty, red-dirt road. So many families are scattered about now, but back then it was a family affair with aunts, uncles, cousins and greats and grands galore. No need to knock, we just barged on in for hugs and helped ourselves to whatever goodies were in arm's reach.

Most afternoons, after a considerable amount of thumping to find the ripest one, PaPa would spread the word among his brood of barefoot grandchildren that he was fixin' to cut a melon. We dropped whatever we were doing and immediately rushed to the shade of the pecan trees in Papa's back yard. We knew the routine well: Retrieve sawhorses and planks from defunct smokehouse. Assemble a makeshift picnic table. Use elbows to gain a strategic spot at table. Wait for PaPa to plunge his knife deep into the heart of the melon. Dive in headfirst.

Table manners didn't apply when it came to watermelon eatin'. The more juice that dripped from our chins and the deeper we buried our faces into the sweet, red pulp, the better. Seeds weren't picked out but used as ammunition in the spitting wars that inevitably broke out at the table. PaPa always warned us, "Don't swallow the seeds! A watermelon will grow in your belly!"

After all the sweetness had been devoured down to the rind, fun was still to be had. PaPa would take his pocketknife and carve each one of us a set of "false teeth" from the remains. Full and content from watermelon and a grandfather's special kind of love, we couldn't wait to see what tomorrow would hold.

Now that I am a grandmother myself, I understand exactly what the "grand" in mother means. My cherished parents, grandparents, many of my aunts and uncles, and even a cousin, have all passed on. They live on in my heart and in the woods, trails, hollows and hallowed earth of Clark Hill.

We didn't have sophisticated gadgets to pass the time, so we made our own fun with family, friends and activities as simple as cutting a melon. It was an age of innocence where Mayberry, Opie, Andy and Lucy set the standard. We could still pray and recite the Pledge of Allegiance at the schoolhouse, and nobody was offended. We are blessed that we had a family who cared and spoiled us only with love. It was all we needed.

AT THE FIVE AND DIME

Nothing was more American in the mid-twentieth century than the five-and-dime store. In fact, no small town was more totally, wonderfully American than Laurel during that same period. For several decades, Woolworth's presided over the corner of Central Avenue and Ellisville Boulevard directly across from Fine Brothers. Both stores still exist so vividly in my memory that I refuse to refer to the buildings as anything but Woolworth's and Fine's.

Every two weeks, as predictable as the rising and setting sun, my father, the sole breadwinner of the household, proudly brought home his paycheck. In turn, my mother, the homemaker, was entrusted to take it to the First National Bank for deposit. This invariably meant that I would have a couple of bucks to throw away on unnecessary paraphernalia such as fake fingernails (those things never stayed on more than ten minutes), rat-tail combs, candy-apple-red nail polish, paddle balls, hula hoops, or maybe even a lavender bottle of not-so-bubbly bubble bath if my heart desired it.

Because of her aversion to parallel parking, my mother would always park our Impala across the train tracks in the lot near Marie's Diner. With my hand safely in hers, I would skip while she strode purposely with her patent leather purse, which held two week's worth of the sweat of my daddy's brow, in the crook of her right elbow.

Crossing the tracks was always a leap of faith even though the coast was clear south towards Ellisville and north to Heidelberg. "You just can't be too careful crossing the train tracks," my mother would warn. Then there was the recurring vision that a train would come screaming out of the distance at the precise moment that one of my Ked's became lodged between the tracks. In a nick of time my mother would untie my shoe, drag me by the arms, and there we would tumble onto the sidewalk unscathed by the roaring train.

Just over the tracks, on cool days we passed by the hobos hovering around a smoky fire warming their hands. "Oh, they are harmless," my mother would declare, but the traffic light could never turn red fast enough for us to get to the other side to Woolworth's. One day the most amazing thing happened. She let go of my hand as she pulled out two wrinkled dollars from her coin purse. "You want to go in Woolworth's by yourself while I walk to the bank? You can sit at the fountain and get yourself a coke and a doughnut if you want it. Wait for me and don't go anywhere else." In that instant she had let go of my hand and given me wings. My first taste of total independence happened at the five-and-dime.

Woolworth's eventually died out along with the hobos and their smoky fires. A few years ago, we did happen upon one in St. Augustine, Florida. It thrilled me so much I just had to belly up to the counter for a doughnut and a Coke with my daughter. I closed my eyes, breathed in deeply and asked her if she smelled it. "Smell what?" She looked completely puzzled. "My childhood," I sighed. It was something like popcorn and bubble gum rubbed together on the bottom of a leather shoe sole.

Part 3:

GROWING UP

southern in the '60s

TRAVELERS IN SEARCH OF VACANCY

This is a semi-true story. I made up a few things, and there's some I'll never forget. The lives and the telling are all very real. They run like the rain in my memory.

We are about to take a trip. It is summer in the dawning of the sixties. The Vietnam War is smoldering on the horizon. J.F.K., M.L.K. and R.F.K. are still alive and hoping to change the world. Man has not yet walked on the moon. Gas stations are still full-service, and attendants will happily look under the hood to check the oil. Gas costs 30 cents a gallon. Cars are still made in America of solid steel and with plenty of power to get you where you are going in a hurry. There is no warning on the packs so people still enjoy cigarettes as if they are actually good for their health.

After great debate, my daddy and his brother have decided that the whole Clark clan will pack up and take a road trip to Florida. With five of us crammed into our freshly waxed Chevrolet and six packed into Uncle Paul's shiny Ford, the two veterans launch our mission with military skill at precisely 0400 hours. If the excitement among us seven kids could be transformed into gasoline, there would be more than enough to propel us all the way to Key West.

I don't ever remember leaving for a vacation in the daylight. The Clark philosophy was that if you left after sunrise, you might as well not go at all. Our two mothers had fried some chicken the night before for a picnic lunch at a roadside park. By 9:00 a.m. we are so hungry we are forced to stop by the side of the road and get that chicken out of the metal ice chest. No food known to man is better than cold, fried chicken served with fresh Sunbeam loaf bread and washed down with an icy Coke in a short bottle. These days, if I had to choose between eating at a five-star restaurant in Manhattan or one of those impromptu picnics beside the road with my family, cold chicken would win hands down. Combine that with the titillating billboards that are beginning to pop up along the way promising adventure, souvenirs, mermaids, oranges, and reptiles, and it is almost more than a young traveler can stand.

By early afternoon, we are deep into the Sunshine State, not the beaches, but the heart of it. You have to remember this was Florida before Mickey Mouse moved in and changed the whole scheme of things. This was Florida the way it still should be, and the way I will always remember it. The two-laned highways snake their way under the canopy of ancient oak trees. We meander through sleepy little towns that are yet oblivious to the impending turnpikes and tourist fantasy worlds that will forever change their way of life.

It is icky hot, and my legs are sticking to the naugehyde seats. Daddy won't run the air-conditioning because he can get better gas mileage that way. He has to prove to his brother that his Chevy will outperform his Ford on the open road so they can argue when we finally get to a stopping point. He has his left arm propped on the window where the wind can blow up his shirtsleeve. Mother is doing the same with her right arm as she takes in the scenery through cat-eye sunglasses. My sisters must be asleep in the backseat because they have finally stopped arguing about who gets to look at that stupid movie star magazine. Who cares about Troy Donahue and Sandra Dee when all I can think about is getting out of this rolling oven into a cool, blue swimming pool? Daddy and Uncle Paul promised we would get a motel with a pool. I say a silent prayer. "Please, please Lord, help them find one soon, and I promise not to beg for a rubber snake at the souvenir shop. Amen."

It is the late afternoon, and it seems my prayer has fallen on deaf ears. We have passed several motels along the road with signs that advertise, AIR-CONDITIONED, T.V., POOL, AND NO VA-CANCY. We are all on the verge of tears at the thought of having to sleep in the car, or worse yet, stay in a motel with no pool. The ones with no pool have a VACANCY sign every time.

Praise the Lord! I see a neon sign down the road that reads VACANCY and POOL. Those two wonderful daddies, dressed in their seersucker Bermuda shorts and dress socks save us from a fate worse than death when they rent the last two rooms available. Way past the orange glow of dusk, we kids splash in the pool while our road-weary parents unwind under oak trees that are dripping with Spanish moss. Patiently watching us from rusty metal lawn chairs, they battle mosquitoes while we fight with each other in the pool. Somebody pinch me. I've died and gone to Heaven, and it's in Florida.

It is the crack of dawn, and Daddy is up and ready to hit the road. He wakes up my sister, Marilyn, and asks her where she packed that white goop that she smears on her face for pimples. It's her Noxzema, and he needs it to cool his left arm, which is sporting 600 miles of sunburn. He is in a hurry to beat the crowd to Silver Springs—home of the world famous glass-bottomed boats.

Before we departed on our cruise, a photographer made a souvenir picture of us, which finally arrived R.F.D. a few weeks later. There we were, seven baby boomers with our faces all in a row, obviously cut from the same genetic material, two war veterans and their lovely stay-at-home wives. We weren't perfect, but it was a perfectly American moment that should have been captured in a Norman Rockwell painting.

The next day we toured Weeki-Wachee and marveled at the live mermaid show presented in a giant aquarium. I almost drowned that night in the pool trying to re-create the performance. Later that day we toured a reptile farm where daring alligator wrestlers defied death by rolling the man eaters onto their backs and then put them to sleep by rubbing their stomachs.

That stop proved quite lucrative for all of us. Phyllis got a stack of wish-you-were-here postcards to mail to her friends back home. Marilyn bought a snow globe that she could shake, and it would appear to be snowing on the tiny beach and palm trees inside. Daddy bought me a scary rubber snake that I didn't even have to beg for. Frank purchased a whoopee cushion that entertained us for the rest of the trip, until Aunt Bobbie sat unawares on it one too many times. If you can name me anything funnier to an eight year old boy than slipping a whoopee cushion into his mother's chair in a restaurant full of diners, I would like to know what it is. She threw it out the window on the way home, somewhere around Pensacola. R.P., my cousin, bought a pack of firecrackers and "accidentally" set them off in the parking lot outside the reptile farm. At that point, the management asked us to please return to Mississippi because it had caused a near disastrous stampede amongst the reptile population.

Before we were asked to leave, a clerk in the shop told us that Walt Disney was planning to build another Disneyland in Florida. Little did we know that Disney would in fact build a fantasy world where real things like alligators and pink flamingos wouldn't be quite so fascinating any more.

There were other trips after that, but each year one more stayed behind as they grew into adulthood. Things definitely changed and even went a little downhill during the years that followed. Our young president was killed in Dallas, abruptly ending that innocent era. R.P. voluntarily joined the Army and fought in a war that none of us understand to this day. One sultry, summer night in 1969 we all gathered around our black and white T.V. and watched Neil Armstrong make a giant leap for mankind. Then came Woodstock and Hurricane Camille. For me and many other Baby Boomers, the summer of '69 was the beginning of the end of the age of innocence.

My Daddy and his brother never stopped arguing, but they learned to appreciate each other's opinion. Five members of the cast of characters, including the parents and R.P., have now passed away. Disney World and its fabricated fun have beckoned my family five times. I still have difficulty accepting the fact that things will never be the same as they were that perfect summer of so long ago.

Childhood memories die hard, especially the perfect, semi-true ones. On road trips, I can't help but smile inside when I catch myself searching for motels with faded, half-lit neon signs that beckon travelers with AIR-CONDITIONED, POOL, T.V. These days, the signs always read VACANCY.

RUNNING WITH SCISSORS

The other day I came across a 60's vintage photo of a cute enough little girl. Without my glasses, I couldn't identify the strange child with the terrible hairdo. It was a color school days photo from Sandersville Elementary School dated 1963-64. A tiny glimpse of a crimson dress visible in the photo jogged my memory. The red dress, innocent face, and the impish smile once belonged to me. The terrible hairdo and the crooked bangs came at the hands of my mother— bless her sweet soul.

For some reason, unbeknownst to me now, my mother became a "kitchen table" beautician. Perhaps she did it out of necessity. When you have four daughters, each with their very own head of hair, professional hair styling was very expensive, even back then.

All of her victims, I mean clients, were close friends, neighbors or family members. She didn't do it for pay but was delighted if they brought her a cutting from the prettiest shrub or flower in their yard. Although she preferred the Lilt brand, her only stipulation was that they bring their own permanent wave kit, and she would furnish everything else needed to turn their stringy, straight hair into tightly wound spit curls.

The ladies came and went as if they were part of some covert operation, their heads concealed by silk scarves or those fancy swim cap coverings adorned with iridescent half-dollar sized sequins. I would eavesdrop on their muffled conversations, "We need to hurry. My husband will be home early today. You know he doesn't approve of this. I'm hoping he won't notice."

Mother would seat them at the kitchen table with a cup of coffee where she practiced her trade. She stored her rollers, papers, scissors, bobby pins, clips and neck clippers in a broken down shoebox. I don't know why to this day, but the contents of that box made me forget all about my Sunday school lessons. Although she had already warned me a thousand times during my short years on the earth not to run with scissors, I'd snatch them from that box and take off running like a demon child through the screen door into the yard. I knew my punishment would be swift and sure. In those days, my mother could move like a gazelle. She would grab the fly swatter off the top of the refrigerator and come after me wielding her punishment with the speed of Zorro.

"You are going to put your eye out if you don't stop running right this second!"

Swoosh, swoosh, swish went the fly swatter, and then it was all over but the crying. In my wildest imaginings, I couldn't figure how running with scissors could end with my living at the school for the blind. I also wondered if she would have still swatted my legs if she had found me standing in the yard with my bloody, blue eyeball in one hand and the culprit scissors in the other.

Several times a year, around Easter, and always the evening before school pictures, it would be my turn to sit at the kitchen table for my "permanent" and the cutting of the bangs ceremony. My mother never did take into consideration that I was afflicted at birth with a cowlick on the right front area of my head. She would press my bangs down with a comb and clip them straight across in the middle of my forehead. Once she lifted the comb, that cowlick would spring back up like a jack-in-the-box. She plastered it with Dippity-Do, taped it with scotch tape overnight, and even tried to tame it with her own saliva, but it was all in vain.

Surely you remember that picture day in elementary school was one of the most exciting days of the school year, and it's importance fell right behind the class Christmas party. We always dressed our very best for picture day—new dress, crinoline slip, and lacy socks topped off with patent leather Mary Jane's. All that fuss was pointless since school pictures showed scarcely more than two inches of the neck of my dress but not a glimpse of the rest of me.

One thing is as true as the blue sky, my mother always made

sure I had a new dress, curly hair and crooked bangs on picture day. The impish grin in the picture was because the night before, when she wasn't looking, I went running with scissors.

BICYCLE SUMMERS

Back in the sixties, when our nine-month sentence in the classroom ended and the shackles of homework fell away, we knew better than to complain of being bored. Uttering that one word within earshot of our parents could get us another three-month sentence in the garden picking butter beans or shucking corn. We didn't know it at the time, but those precious summer days filled with vivid imaginations, riding bicycles and exploring the outdoors, became the marker by which we judged the summers that followed. No matter how hard we try to retrieve that summer solstice magic and convey it to our children, it comes up short and hokey. Those summers were like fireflies in a mason jar—they twinkled and glowed for a little while and then they were gone.

The boredom antidotes that kids enjoy today would have been science-fiction back then. Instead of I-pods containing play lists of hundreds of favorite songs, we had a short stack of scratched 45's and never even listened to the flipside. Because of party phone lines, we had to wait until all the neighborhood gossip had been broadcast up and down the wires eight times before we could call our friends. If the Cubans had fired a nuclear weapon at Florida, we wouldn't have known about it until the next day because the paper came via mail a day after the fact. We owned a Kodak Instamatic camera, but it still took two weeks for us to see the results. Most of the time, the subjects were off-center and headless. Photography was often a roll of the dice with some hilarious results. In an old shoebox, I found a photo of me standing in front of the Washington Monument. Preserved for all eternity, is my toothless head at the bottom of the photo with that white obelisk protruding from my cranium like a giant unicorn horn.

If the class smarty pants had told the class bully that in the year 2007, we would be able to take pictures with a portable phone and send it magically through the air to another phone, he would have gotten his nose busted for fibbin.' Kids born in the fifties adhered to the long-held belief that "good things come to those who wait." This younger generation's motto could be "we expect every good thing instantly." Everybody likes instant gratification, but it's killing our patience and imagination.

If we waited patiently, did our appointed chores and didn't

slam the screen door too much, we were treated to the ultimate summer pleasure--swimming once a week at Lake Bounds or Lake Waukaway. The remaining days of the week we didn't know where we would go, but it was always our imaginations and bicycles that took us there. Our days began while the grass was still wet with dew and didn't end until the lightning bugs signaled that it was time to go inside.

Inspired by the books we had read or the television shows of that era, our imaginations took us anywhere we wanted to go. We became Tom and Huck without a river, John Glenn without a rocket, Little Joe Cartwright without a horse and Gilligan without an island. Some days we would strike out east toward the county line to the launching pad at Cape Canaveral (the oil tanks) or west to the Mississippi River (Bogue Homa Creek) to throw rocks at the man-eating reptiles (snakes and turtles). We were marooned on an island and tried to build an escape raft to cross the ocean (my grandfather's pond). During that adventure, Gilligan (my cousin) chopped Ginger's (me) big toe half into with a hatchet and then became Dr. Kildare for a couple weeks.

When we got thirsty, we would peddle down to the Fountain of Youth (artesian well) at the old Bryan schoolhouse. We knelt down prayerfully and drank that magical water until our sides hurt. We truly believed that we would never grow old and that the summer would never end. September always came. In fact, more than forty summers came and went quicker than a bicycle ride down Clark Hill. Looking back now, maybe we just didn't drink enough of that water.

WISHES CAN COME TRUE

On January 19th, 2008, all of Jones County awakened to a surprise and were given the opportunity to make memories that will last a lifetime. As I looked out my kitchen window that morning, an unfamiliar, white peacefulness blanketed my yard and warmed my heart. My thoughts turned to the people, the times, and the place where I built my first snowman many years ago. To accurately recapture that part of my childhood for this narrative, I was compelled to go home emotionally and physically to build my second snowman.

As most children do, I spent a fair amount of time wishing for things I would never have. At a very young age, I went through a phase where I wished to fly like Tinker Bell. In my dreams it felt so effortless and real—sort of like a frog swimming through the air instead of water. It didn't take but one leap out of the fork of the Chinaberry tree in my granddaddy's yard to put that wish to rest. Later on, I turned my sights toward more realistic wishes such as marrying Elvis and singing like Patsy Cline. Those didn't pan out either. Every summer, I wished that my parents wouldn't prod me onto that big, yellow bus in September, which was as preposterous as wishing to fly. Once back in school, I wished for December to come with great haste. Each Christmas, I wished so hard that my head hurt that it would be white so we could dash through the snow in a one-horse, open sleigh then stroll through the meadow and build a snowman. Just like all my other wishes, they were futile. Instead of giving up on the wish altogether, I made concessions based upon my own feasibility study. Since the climate in Mississippi is so fickle in winter and there was always a 50/50 chance that I'd be wearing shorts to Christmas dinner, I simply wished to build a snowman just once in my life. The day or month became negotiable. Secure in the knowledge that my wish was a feasible one, I waited.

Sometime during the winter of 1964, an event of astonishing proportions took place. The wise man that he was, my granddaddy surveyed the cloud formations and predicted snow flurries. When the heavy clouds opened up, what fell from the sky that day was beyond our wildest dreams. That was the day that I first counted the six points of a snowflake in my hand.

It wasn't just a flurry as my granddaddy predicted. It fell from the sky for hours. Some flakes were fluffy like cotton balls, while others were like B-Bs that stung our cheeks when they landed. We ran into the yard celebrating wildly and sank to our knees in disbelief. We stuck out our tongues and let the flakes light there for a fleeting second until they melted. It is a moment in time that is forever frozen in my memory.

We were children of the snow-barren South who dwelled only eighty miles from the Gulf of Mexico. We were barefoot scholars of summertime living, but highly illiterate in the practice of bundled-up wintertime frolicking. We were bike-riding, Moon-Pie-eating, peach-Nehi-guzzlers who had only sang about or seen in Christmas cards the joy that was falling upon our heads. A mitten was just a cute word that rhymed with kitten. We had never seen a pair of ice skates, snow skis or a sled. We had roasted plenty of wieners and marshmallows on an open fire but weren't quite sure about chestnuts.

When we were finished building him, we knew all too well that he was a mortal snowman and that his life would melt away before our very eyes. I mourned on the second day after his creation when his head tumbled into the yard. We desperately tried to revive him, but all the other snow that had given him life had disappeared. His headless remains lingered shrinking for several days until we came home from school one sunny afternoon to find that our snowman had vanished into the brown grass of the yard. He was the first, and last Saturday, "Jack" the snowman (as in a Jack-in-the-box surprise), was the second that I ever helped create. The first is eternally frozen in black and white photos and stored in an old shoebox, and the last is immortalized in living color and set to a soundtrack on

DVD.

When the snowfall subsided, it occurred to me that my grown-up reaction to it was no less exuberant than it was when I was eight and seeing it for the very first time. I'll always cherish those two days when nature granted my childhood wish and then amazed me by granting it again forty-four years later. Considering my record of fulfilled wishes and the latitude of this state I call home, twice in a lifetime ain't half bad.

THE OLD SWIMMING HOLE

Before Lake Waukaway, there was Lake Bounds. I cannot write my memoirs of one without remembering the other as they are both forever intertwined in my life as a Southern child. An edited version of this column first appeared in the July 2000 edition of *Country Extra* magazine, a national publication with a circulation of two million.

Of all the pleasures of my barefoot summer days growing up in Mississippi, going swimming was the sweetest.

There were no swimming pools for us kids back then. But, we could always count on Aunt Beck (Becky Clark Gooch of the Bethel community and of Clark Hill) to save us from our misery when she'd load us into Jezebel, her 1941 Mercury, and set out for a place God made just for children with dusty feet and a few hours to kill.

Aunt Beck would announce a day or two in advance when she would be going to Lake Bounds—and the word traveled fast. When the day and the hour finally arrived, we donned our swimsuits and slung our gear into Jezebel's massive trunk. One by one, we piled into the car, taking our places on Jezebel's scratchy wool seats. Arguments always erupted over who'd get the coveted window seats. Being one of the younger kids, I was exiled to the center where my legs were wedged together and stuck fast to the passenger beside me.

Our journey normally started out with about seven passengers, but we usually picked up one or two more barefoot children down the road. By the time we crossed the Wayne county line, we were a rolling inferno with sweat pouring from our faces. Oh no, we didn't mind at all because it was summer in Mississippi, and we were going swimming!

Despite her heavy load, Jezebel climbed Rock Hill like a champion, maneuvered the dusty back roads and passed clickitty-clack over the wooden bridge at the fork in the road. Once we reached Eucutta, the road mercifully changed to blacktop. As she left an orange cloud of dust in her wake, Aunt Beck opened up ole Jezebel like she was on her final lap at Talladega.

Nestled in a hollow surrounded by virgin pines, Lake Bounds appeared approximately the size of Lake Superior to us kids. The deep water in the middle was a foreboding green, while the shallow water was crystal clear—the color of a green Coca-Cola bottle.

Jezebel's doors flew open and children fled from the four-wheeled oven even before it came to a dead stop. We raced furiously to the water with our feet kicking up sand, because "the last one in was a rotten egg."

It was impossible to leisurely stroll into Lake Bounds. Springs deep in the earth fed the lake with water so unbelievably cold that it turned our lips blue. We simply held our breath and plunged in, popping up like corks and screaming in delight at the wonder of it all.

Every minute at the lake was precious and fleeting. We wished for time to stand still or at least creep at a turtle's pace as we swam, soaked up the Mississippi sun, picnicked on fried chicken and gorged on watermelon until we thought we would burst.

Every hour or so Aunt Beck forced us out of the water for thawing and refueling. The old country store and gristmill was the perfect place to raise our body temperature to an acceptable 98.6 degrees. I can still feel my bare feet against the gritty wooden floors and crave the taste of a Zero candy bar washed down with the refreshing burn of a Dr. Pepper.

As the sunlight began to slant across the water, we knew that we would soon have to surrender our fun to the sunset. Then came my aunt's first half-hearted warning shot followed by a more stern second and then the third and final, "If you don't get out of the water this second, I'm leaving without you!"

With pouting purple lips and rosy cheeks, we reluctantly plopped into the car and began our trip home. No sweating or sticking to each other now because we were living, breathing popsicles.

Our excitement was replaced with a satisfied brand of exhaustion that kept us at peace with each other and ourselves all the way home.

The lake is deserted now. The sisters who ran it died more years ago than I can recall.

I miss what Lake Bounds represented to us kids of that generation. I miss it for my children and the grandchildren that will one day come along. They will never experience the thrill of swimming in that special place and being a child in that simpler time. I wish they could have. I really do.

A SUMMER PLACE

It's mid July and the humidity is adding weight to the heavy feeling that another summer is passing me by. The 4th of July came and went without so much as a firecracker exploding at my house. Holidays propel themselves toward me at warp speed, catching me off guard and ill-prepared for celebrations that the calendar says I should commemorate. Often, I feel like Han Solo dodging imperial cruisers, but somehow emerge unscathed but addled on the other side with nothing but a pile of dirty dishes as evidence that a celebration took place.

Summertime of my teens—summers without responsibilities and bursting with possibilities—is what I need now. Whatever happened to those cut-off shorts so frayed that the front pockets peeked out, dime store flip flops, my tan firm thighs, Sun-In hair highlighter and that baby oil and iodine concoction that tinted my skin the color of a wheat penny? When did we stop those urgent trips to our "summer place" with our feet tapping the dashboard to "Sittin' on the Dock of the Bay"? How do I not remember the exact moment that the music faded, and I began looking at those seemingly endless summer days not over the hood of a '64 Pontiac but through the rearview mirror?

After the lake closed years ago, it was sold and re-opened as a reservations-only, Christian retreat. With the summer heat weighing heavy now, the lake is all I have been able to think about. I wonder how time has marred our exalted summer place—the hills, the woods, the trails, and the water—especially the water.

It is strange how much you can remember about places like that once you allow yourself to return. You remember one thing, and that instantly reminds you of another and then another. I remember clearest of all the coldness of the water, children bounding down boardwalks that surrounded the lake, and the four-platform diving tower. I was too chicken to jump from the pinnacle and always promised myself to do it the next time. Performing a belly-buster off the lowest platform and finding my bikini top floating on top of the water together comprise the most daring and embarrassing feat of my life.

Then, I remembered the proprietor, Mr. Allen, lounging on the counter, shirtless and completely elated to see each and every patron that descended the rocky stairway into his haven of bliss.

Now, I remember the smell of popcorn served up in colorful paper cones and snow cones that turned my lips blue or red or purple. Boys. Yes, there were sun-kissed jocks who appeared to be auditioning for Charles Atlas ads. Girls. There were giggling, bikini-clad girls perched flirtingly in the sun looking to see if the guys were looking to see them. Boy plus girl plus music multiplied by sun equaled the promise of summer romances and stolen kisses on the nature trails. Ahhh, I get chills from the scent of Coppertone suntan lotion, the original white potion that subtracts forty years from my life when I rub it on. Music. There was always music echoing off the water into my heart--the greatest hits from the greatest decade that music has ever known.

It's perplexing how all the sights, scents and sounds are so clear, but words to describe the sensation of plunging into the frigid water elude me now.

My recollections of Lake Waukaway have now become so exaggerated in my mind that I am afraid if I ever return they will disappoint me. It seems to me as I remember all this, that those times and our summer place were indeed rare and worthy of exaggeration. I have tried to remember the last time that I swam in the lake. I'm not sure if it was the summer before my senior year or the summer after, in 1973, when I spent a heartbroken 4th of July with my best "friend boy" after a break-up with my steady boyfriend. He is now deceased, but I still see his freckled face in the golden light of that summer day and hear his gallant promise to marry me if no one else would.

Regardless of the year, I now realize my last trip to the lake represented a passage that should have been put on paper somewhere for safekeeping. When we were young and caught up in the moment, we believed that age would never catch up with us. I guess it's a good thing that we don't know when we are doing something for the last time. If I had known then what I know now, I would have climbed to the very top of the diving tower, closed my eyes and jumped just so my memories could be complete.

A ROAD RAN THROUGH IT

On a spring-like winter day while visiting my sister, I took a senti-
mental journey across a forbidden road into my aunt's front yard.
Something in the air caused a flood of memories to wash over me.
Those memories were as warm as an April sun, and for a few seconds
I stood there totally immersed in what was once a field of dreams.

You see, my boy cousins and their friends played Little
League baseball. Therefore, I desperately wanted to be a baseball
player too. Little girls of my generation weren't allowed to play
organized baseball and certainly not encouraged to participate in any
competitive sport outside of school-sponsored athletics. Back then,
most girls wanted to be pretty and studious, but not athletic.

Afraid to cross the road, I stood at the end of our driveway and told them I wanted to practice with them. Reluctantly, they huddled, took a secret vote and decided to put me in the outfield, mainly because they were a "man" short. All the boys were quite impressed that I didn't lob the ball daintily like a girl from behind my ear in a high arc. I threw it side-armed, snappy and confident, as they did. My less desirable position in left field really didn't matter to me at the time because it was competitive and tons more fun than playing paper dolls.

When they didn't have regular practice or games, we converged on the only logical playing field available—my aunt's front yard. The pitcher's mound wasn't a mound at all, and the elevation of the yard placed it several degrees lower than home plate. The bases were merely bare spots in the yard that spawned many an argument about the safe or out condition of base runners. There was one more slight problem with our field. The road from Sandersville to Eucutta ran smack dab through the middle of the outfield.

From the day I was old enough to walk, my mother had an intense fear of my crossing the road and getting run over. As a result, I spent an unnecessary amount of time dreaming up ways to sneak across undetected, knowing with certainty that she would blister my legs with a switch if she caught me. Over all the years since I left my mother's care, I have yet to cross a road or street without hearing these ten words of impending doom ringing in my head: "Don't' cross the road! You know you'll get run over!!"

My aunt didn't seem to worry that much about her three sons as they spent half their childhoods roaming about in the middle of the road. It's not surprising that the boys seldom crossed over to my side because nothing that interested them abided there. All we had to offer was nail polish, sponge rollers, or Maybelline eyeliner. For me, it was quite the opposite. All the forbidden fruits of my girlhood dwelled across that forbidden road at their house.

How I loved the feel and the smell of a leather baseball glove on my hand and the sound a bat made when I hit the ball just right. I liked the fact that even though I wore ruffled things and took bubble baths, I could still hit, throw and run with the boys.

Eventually, after my mother grew tired of cutting switches, she surrendered to her fears.

On that imperfect field in that perfect time of our lives, we simply played the game of baseball. In the process we learned a whole lot about life: Not everyone is meant to be a star. You can't win them all. Girls can be just as competitive as boys. Some people are born wimps. Being part of a team makes you feel special. Namecalling leaves a bad taste in your mouth. A few people really deserve to be hit in the head with a bat. Having the wind knocked out of you with a fastball is tough. It's even tougher to suck it up, shake it off and keep on playing through the tears.

That day while reminiscing in our abandoned field of dreams, I was compelled to take a batter's stance between the two towering pine trees where the boys and one girl of summer celebrated a thousand home runs. My mind's eye saw the most perfect pitch that had ever been thrown. I swung my imaginary bat mightily then heard the sweet sound of wood pounding leather. My heart leaped as the ball sailed up, up and over the road into left field. There were no

cars coming from either direction as I ran from base to base, deliber-
ately tagging each one with my right foot until I crossed home plate
one last time.

POSTCARD MEMORIES

Before the days of interstate travel, cross-country travel was conducted on a series of two-lane federal highways. A few miles north of Sandersville, along the picturesque hills and valleys my daddy always referred to as the foothills of the foothills of the Smokey Mountains, US-11 passes through a largely forgotten utopia named Stafford Springs. As a child, I knew or cared nothing of its historical significance and that the water bubbling up from the earth was once considered therapeutic. No one ever mentioned that visitors from all over the country journeyed there at the turn of the 20th Century to convalesce in the modern hotel and to partake of its highly acclaimed healing powers. My recent research revealed that the Choctaw Indians native to this area named the water "Bogahoma" or "Water of Life," and that many of those who drank it appeared to profit some relief.

As a grade school girl, Stafford Springs was an unattainable haven of bliss in my own back yard, a constant source of longing and curiosity about the fortunate ones who parked their station wagons in front of the air-conditioned motor cottages, splashed in the pool's chlorine-spiked waters, and rode horseback on the wooded trails of the Dude Ranch. This question was never asked of my daddy but loomed large and logical in my young mind, "Why must we travel for hours to another vacation destination when we could stay there, save time, money and not wear out the new Impala?"

This smoldering remembrance of Stafford Springs was fueled by a copy of a few vintage postcards obtained by one of my co-workers. The collage has been sitting by my computer for several weeks now. I've studied them briefly each morning in an attempt to place myself accurately in them and have waited patiently until now for the words to seep up from the springs of my own imagination.

It is a blistering hot summer day in 1966 as I gaze up at the clouds and the yellow pines towering in the haze. I am floating in the shallow end of the pool inside an old tire inner tube, being particular not to let the air valve scratch my ribs. A young woman in a black, Catalina one-piece is posed on the back of the diving board while another is poised to take a dive off the end. Two older couples all the way from New Jersey are unwinding in aluminum folding chairs. I strain my ears to translate, and think to myself, they talk fast like 33 R.P.M. albums on a record player set at 45 R.P.M., while people around here talk just the opposite. Both the men are savoring the benefits of a cigarette while their wives are drinking that new Tab diet drink that tastes like Vicks 44 cough syrup to me. They are mapping out a journey that will take them to New Orleans and then on to the Houston Astrodome for an indoor baseball game. Two prissy teenaged girls are sunning on chaise lounge chairs and trying to tune a static-filled transistor radio. They want to listen to some Beatles or Rolling Stones music, but the signal keeps fading in and out. One of them laments that she misses her boyfriend and is going to call him on the pay phone if she can round up enough change. I wish I never had to leave this place.

In 1967, I-59 opened and nailed the coffin shut on the Stafford Springs resort, burying my fantasy of vacationing in my own back yard. Although my family did enjoy many Sunday meals in the restaurant, I never so much as dipped a toe in the swimming pool or took a peek inside one of the motor cottages.

The interstate paved the way for speed, progress, chain motels and fast-food restaurants. Thankfully, smoking became taboo because of the Surgeon General's warning on every pack. Since then, it's been a "long and winding road" for the Beatles, and the geriatric Rolling Stones really "can't get no satisfaction." There are now a hundred different brands of diet drinks that actually don't taste like cough syrup. The Astrodome, which was once nicknamed the Eighth Wonder of the World, is in danger of being torn down. Everyone knows what Katrina did to New Orleans. Primitive transistor radios and record players can be found in antiques stores. All of we prissy young girls are now eligible for the A.A.R.P. I can't remember the last time I even saw a pay phone.

Although the Bogue Homa waters are still flowing, virtually nothing tangible remains of Stafford Springs but a fading restaurant sign and a sparsely traveled stretch of Highway 11.

All I have are these imaginary postcard memories and the haunting dream of summers past spent vacationing in my own backyard.

SEE THE U.S.A. IN YOUR CHEVROLET

With the state of the nation and the economy in an unrecognizable condition from the America our parents knew during the post-war years, my husband and I always ask out loud after hearing more disturbing news, "I wonder what James and Ralph would think about that?" Because they are still very much with us, we refer to our fathers by their first names because it just doesn't seem right to say Daddy in the past tense. They were two like-minded men of the same generation, born a year apart, who survived the Great Depression, served honorably in World War II, proudly came home, then poured every ounce of determination and sweat in their being into forging a good life for their families. They expected absolutely nothing in return except life, liberty and the pursuit of happiness. That included no handouts, bailouts, tax breaks or free lunches.

We concurred that they both would have gone along with the premise of bank bailouts because loans have always been necessary for the country to grow and prosper. Very few returning soldiers could have purchased a home, car or started a business without a little help from the banks. They probably would have had a few choice words about greedy, free-spending corporations being bailed out because they are too big to fail. Their concern would be more about the failure of little men such as themselves who are the glue that holds this country together.

With last week's news that General Motors had filed for Chapter 11 bankruptcy after our government had already tried to revive them with billions upon billions of our tax dollars—earned by the sweat of their brows and at the expense of their aching backs, not to mention their undying loyalty to GM products, we are convinced that both of them must be spinning in their graves. I almost called my sister and asked her to walk up to Bethel Cemetery to see if my daddy had not resurrected himself and made his way to Detroit or Washington to get some answers to the question all of us are asking. What in the heck happened to baseball, hot dogs, apple pie and Chevrolet?

In the 1950's, Dinah Shore sang the second national anthem, "See the U.S.A. in Your Chevrolet." See it, we did--from sea to shining sea! Ralph purchased a red Bel Air sedan in 1957, ran the wheels off it, and then traded for a new one every couple of years until he switched to Impalas in the mid-sixties. That first Bel Air was a trophy that Ralph pampered like a beautiful woman until he got her on the road, where he would drive her like a bad girl running from the law. The roof was white and the body had the signature white inset swooping back to the rear tail fin. The solid chrome front grill had a wide-open grin that ate up the road and seemed to be saying "make way for a Chevrolet!" Ralph polished the chrome to a mirror finish, making sure to put an extra spit shine on the signature Chevrolet logo. Somewhere in the depths of my memory is a vision of my mother applying her lipstick and patting down her windblown hair while using the rear bumper as a mirror.

A few miles across the county, James had an affinity for GM's Pontiac Catalina. He likewise traded for a new one every couple of years until he bought his last one in 1964. That is the one that whisked me away on my first date in 1970 and was the subject of one of my favorite columns ever. She is still with us today, and just last fall stole my daughter away to her honeymoon. For the next couple of decades, James stayed faithful to the GM brand and would park nothing but slightly used Cadillacs and "like a rock" Chevy trucks in his driveway.

Until recently, Americans have always had a human-like affection for and undying loyalty to their automobiles. Something happened to us, and even I, whose every endearing memory is permeated by the GM car I was riding in at the time, have lost that loving feeling.

Family vacations...first dates...first car purchased as a married couple...second car...third car...brought babies home in car...first baby wrecked first car...first and second babies married and drove away in cars...drove to parents' funerals in cars...Even though many of my unforgettable life experiences involved a GM car, today I drive a Toyota 4-Runner, and my husband drives a Honda Civic. We feel no loyalty or affection for either one of them like we do for the 1964 Catalina or that 1977 Pontiac Grand Prix that rushed me to the hospital when I went into labor—the classic one that we wish desperately we still owned.

I'm still trying to figure out what happened to the iconic General Motors that James and Ralph and many of us once so faithfully pledged our allegiance.

Did GM leave us, or did we leave them?

DON'T TAKE MY KODACHROME AWAY

It was the world's first commercially successful color film, immortalized by Paul Simon's song in 1973: "They give us those nice bright colors. They give us the greens of summers. Makes you think all the world's a sunny day...So, Mama, don't' take my Kodachrome away." When I heard the news that the Eastman Kodak Company would retire Kodachrome, its oldest film stock, because of declining customer demand, I felt like an old friend had passed away.

All of the more memorable instants of my life and many of the mundane moments were captured on Kodachrome film. In fact, an entire dresser in an upstairs bedroom is heavy with dozens of envelopes full of colored snapshots of my past life. Half a dozen photo albums, thick with memories that I can't recall without their assistance, are stored in bookcases upstairs. During the early years of our marriage and when the children came along, I was diligent to near obsession in recording every moment for posterity. Kodachrome and I were there documenting our life through the lenses of an Instamatic camera when we brought them home, when they were toddling or falling down or laughing or crying. Kodak was there with us for every first in my children's lives...birthdays, Mickey Mouse, swimming, sand castles, Christmas, T-ball, ballet, Trick-or-Treating...not one moment went undocumented. It was a labor of love to trudge to the store, decide on the number of exposures needed to adequately capture the event and assure that the camera batteries wouldn't die in the middle of blowing out birthday candles or opening presents. Then, there was the sweet anticipation after mailing the rolls of film to distant laboratories, entrusting strangers with the exalted duty of sending those precious moments back to me in living color.

Kodachrome was also there, sometimes unaware, to capture special moments that proved to be the lasts and onlys that we had no idea were happening before our very eyes...Papaw's last Easter in 2000...the only picture of my daddy's weathered hands...Christmas of 1991 in the old house... the picture of my mother, her siblings and parents taken together at a family reunion in the late '70s. When looking at those pictures now, I am acutely aware that one day my family will see the last picture taken of me.

Kodachrome was not only the basis for my life's story but for the unforgettable images of countless families all over this country. It enjoyed its heyday in the 1950s and '60s when Americans were at their sentimental best. We became mobile and extensively well traveled, hitting the roads for family vacations, never leaving home without a camera and Kodachrome film. That yellow box and trademark red "K" became such an integral part of the American experience that theme parks and tourist attractions had kiosks and shops solely dedicated to the supply and demand of memory keeping with film. It was the medium of choice for countless family slide shows but also for world-renowned images, including Abraham Zapruder's 8-milliter reel of President John F. Kennedy's assassination on November 22, 1963. Later, it was the film of choice on family vacations to Dallas and Washington, D.C. as we captured images of the crime scene and the eternal flame on J.F.K's grave. The assassination of our president was so unbelievable that my daddy was compelled to make those pilgrimages and to see proof with his own eyes and capture it on Kodachrome film.

I can't remember the last time I sent a roll of film to be developed. Thanks to digital cameras, we can capture a moment on a tiny card and then see the results instantly. If we don't like the results, we can simply abort the image and take another until everything is picture perfect. Unforgettable moments of our lives can now be Photo-shopped, Snapfished and Facebooked instantaneously to anyone in the world who has a computer and the Internet.

Sadly, after 74 years, Kodachrome has now gone the way of phone booths, drive-in theaters, eight-track tapes and DVDs.

Call me old fashioned, but I miss the excitement of waiting a few days to see those snippets of my life for the first time on glossy paper that I can hold in my hands and later revisit in a tangible photo album. Pictures of life's greatest moments, until the advent of modern technology, have always been perfectly imperfect. They were often off center, blurred or dimly lit; and its subjects commonly suffered from red eyes, distorted faces, chopped heads and horrible hair. It seems that all of the dramatic so-called improvements have come at a cost. Along the way, we have lost our appreciation for imperfection and have come to expect instant gratification.

I'm sure the quality of life is better now. At least, that's what they keep telling me.

OLD CHEERLEADERS NEVER DIE,
THEY JUST LOSE THEIR MOVES

As you are reading this, young spirit leaders all across the county are zealously preparing for pep rallies and the Friday night-lights of grid-iron sidelines. This column is for them and for every old cheerleader who ever yelled "Two Bits."

In 1967, the year I entered junior high at Northeast Jones High School, female students were not allowed to wear pants. There was no such thing as a blow dryer or panty hose. Ambush was my favorite perfume of all time. Brut cologne worn by certain broad-shouldered athletes made me weak in the knees. My favorite song was "I'm a Believer," by the Monkees. The hippy influence that originated at Haight-Ashbury in San Francisco was on a fast train from California to the hallways of NEJ. As a result, hemlines would become shorter and men's hair would grow longer. The hippies, whose mantra was to "never trust anyone over thirty," are now twice that age themselves. What a humbling reality check that is for us old cheerleaders who could once cartwheel the entire length of a football field.

The first day of school I signed up for band because I wanted to follow in my sisters' footsteps and become a majorette. From the time I could prance about, I had my own baton and majorette boots complete with tassels that swung whimsically as I marched through the kitchen with my imaginary band. My sisters taught me their routines in the front yard, and the baton soon became a semi-permanent extension of my right arm. Being a majorette required playing a musical instrument, so I chose the saxophone because my daddy liked to listen to Boots Randolph.

There was only one problem with my playing the saxophone, which no one ever bothered to mention. One had to have some musical aptitude. I had NONE—ZERO, ZIP. After six fruitless months of blowing sounds that were eerily similar to those of a dying elephant, I realized that flaming batons, sequined costumes and the fanfare of parades were not in the cards for me. The band director would surely be brokenhearted at the loss of such a genetically blessed, albeit musically challenged majorette. His reaction was not quite what I expected. He broke into a lip-ripping smile and in relief said, "Thank God." There ended my dream of being a twirler.

With my less than illustrious band career behind me, new

dreams of pom-poms, pleated skirts and megaphones came true with cheerleader tryouts in the spring of 1968. Cheerleading in the sixties and seventies was so different than it is today. The concept of cheerleaders tumbling and stunting was in its infancy; so we taught ourselves to flip and flop in our backyards with no instruction from trained professionals. I wear a stainless steel screw in my left ankle as a testament. Back in the day, anyone with school spirit and a smile could become a cheerleader. Now, they spend hours in the gym practicing dangerous stunts that literally make your heart stop. They perfect movements that this old cheerleader can't even comprehend, much less execute. They are choreographed dancers, moving parts of the human anatomy that I never knew could move. In 1968, we could freely kick up pointed toes over our heads and move our arms sharply with bladed hands, but our hips and pelvis' were to remain stationary at all times. The slightest suggestive movement in that anatomical area would win you a free trip to the principal's office on Monday morning.

All of us have recollections of our high school days, some more glorious than others. My memories of high school are interwoven with the spirit, smells, sounds, and emotions of pep rallies and ballgames. For me, high school is a menagerie of fading black and gold moments that sit prominently on my mantle of memories. They are permeated with the scent of damp grass, perspiration, liniment, stale gymnasiums, crepe paper, magic markers, and popcorn. They are soaked with the salty tears of defeat and sweaty hugs from all the players after a victory. In them, bass drums reverberate, cymbals clash, and shrill voices scream for the Tiger fans to, "GIVE

ME A T!!!"

Regrets? I never experienced the thrill of tossing a silver baton high into the sky and catching it behind my back on the 50-yard line at halftime. Sadly, I didn't realize how unburdened and magical high school was until it was over. Despite my increasingly immobile joints—the results of years of repeated injuries, broken bones and contortions of the vertebral column—I still wouldn't trade one shining moment in front of the home crowd for a stadium full of saxophones.

The next time you attend a football game, make it a point to watch the cheerleaders. Cheer with them and let them know you appreciate all their hard work and dedication. They are as much the athlete as the young warriors who play the game every Friday night. One day they will be forced to hang up their pom-poms, but they will discover, as I have, that old cheerleaders never die, they just lose their moves.

Part 4:

GETTING BETTER,

not older, with friends

FRIENDS, GOOD FRIENDS,
AND WALLPAPER FRIENDS

My long-time friend and former golfing accomplice called me a couple of weeks ago to inform me that Mr. J, the old tightwad, had finally agreed to remodel their home.   Mrs. J was exuberant, "It's amazing how knocking out a wall can open up a room, and you will just love the countertops I picked out." Before we hung up she hesitated, "Oh, I need you to do me a BIG favor. I want you to hang some wallpaper in the dressing area of the master bath. You are the only one I trust to do it."

The first thought to pop into my head flew right out of my mouth, "Have you lost your mind?! We could pull the old paper down and paint it in thirty minutes." It was apparent that she had rehearsed. "Well, that last layer of Williamsburg floral you hung in '98 peeled off smooth as silk. That horrid mauve and blue paisley flame stitch from '92 gave me fits. I don't know why you let me hang it in the first place. Anyway, the 1984 psychedelic peacock pattern came down in spots but took big chunks out of the sheetrock. What we have now is a "problem" wall, and I bought some neutral, faux-plaster paper that's supposed to remedy this pitiful situation."

Every inch of my being was screaming nooooooo, but thirty years of friendship made me say yes. After all, this desperate woman on the other end of the airwaves went into labor after flipping out of a floating lounge chair in my pool. This woman was the first one at the E.R. when my son totaled his car and the first one I called when my parents passed away. She is the only woman I know who appreciates and can match the best belch I've got. We have a pact that if one of us goes under anesthesia the other will be there in recovery as a safeguard just in case we start spilling our guts of some of the secrets we share. Together, we have danced at weddings, prayed at funerals, cried until we laughed, and laughed until we cried. Sure, I will hang one more era of wallpaper for her.

When I was younger, I believed in the concept of one best friend. Now, that I am older I have come to believe that friends come in degrees. Friends, for instance, could be those people who knew you way back in high school when you parted your mousey, brown hair down the middle and wore too much blue eye shadow. You might have cheered, danced or twirled with them. You possibly double-dated and compared kisses at a pajama party afterwards. It's a bit awkward when you run into them in the grocery store checkout line and they swear you haven't changed a bit in thirty years. You aren't sure if it's a compliment or an insult. When they walk away, you just know they are thinking how flabby your thighs are.

Good friends could be those from college who were attendants in your wedding who you assumed would always be part of your life. Or maybe they are former neighbors who helped you through the childrearing years. They move away or for no particular reason you lose touch, and before you know it, months turn into years and then one day you receive an invitation to their daughter's wedding. You are not surprised to be invited because you remember the day that little girl was born and taught her how to ride a bicycle when she wore a ponytail wrapped in a big pink ribbon. At her wedding, you pick up where you left off, and all those years melt away like warm candle wax.

Wallpaper friends, or whatever you prefer to call them, are the most rare. If you have more than one of them, consider yourself blessed. They might be the ones who forced you to get out of bed when your broken heart told you to stay home in your pajamas and eat fudge rounds all day. Wallpaper friends are the ones who turn on the lights at the end of your tunnel. They will help you tie a knot at the end of your rope and tell you to hang on for dear life. They have probably been unfortunate enough to see you naked and don't care if you've got varicose veins the size of pencils or that your derriere jiggles like a tub of Jell-O. Wallpaper friends look past all that superficial stuff and see into your heart, and like your derriere, sometimes it ain't pretty, but they love you anyway.

Last week, I took my paper-hanging tools over to Mrs. J's and hung her wallpaper for the very last time. Friendship does have its limits. Like the other times before, we ran out with one stinking piece to go. Before we covered that paperless spot, we took a marker and scrawled "Karen and Cheryl were here in 1984, 1992, 1998, 2007. WFF."

WAITING FOR MY STIMULUS MONEY

After wondering and wondering what the new stimulus package of 2009 would do for average Americans, I finally found the answer Saturday night on the Fox Network. During his weekly talk/variety show, former presidential candidate, Mike Huckabee of Arkansas, was discussing the amount with his audience. Some analysts with a lot more time on their hands and a higher aptitude for ciphering than me actually came up with a dollar amount. It was a good bit less than the $130,000 I had calculated so confidently in my tiny right-brained head. After the numbers bounced around inside my skull like silver balls in an old pool hall pinball machine, the lights kept flashing until I had way too many zeroes on the end.

Before I tell you what to expect in your very own wallet, let me go back to the frantic phone call I received from my good friend, Mrs. J.

She was in our favorite store, Dirt Cheap — a.k.a. Earth Chic to the B.B.B.B — Blonde Bombshell Bargain Babes, and called me in a tizzy to inform me that all the attractive women in America would soon be reduced to hagginess if something didn't happen to reverse this recession. She was especially concerned about the exorbitant cost of hair dye, under-eye concealer, razor blades and wrinkle cream, and her ability to continue purchasing them as part of her regular beauty routine. Then she added that our legislators better hurry and get some dollars into the hands of all American women or they would soon find themselves without a single attractive woman to chase up and down the halls of freedom. If that happens, if it hasn't already, our democracy will implode and nothing constructive will ever come out of Washington again. I thought that was pretty profound thinking on the part of Mrs. J—the Queen of Earth Chic.

My suggestion to her was to go with the generic brands because they are reported to be basically the same as the name brands found at better department stores such as Saks and Bloomingdales. My left ear might be permanently damaged from her reaction to that sage advice. In essence, what she shrieked into my ear was that you couldn't get any cheaper than the bargain bin at Dirt Cheap. Then she asked how I thought she might look with midnight blue hair, because she could get as much of that color hair dye as she could haul out of the store for 50 cents a bottle. And, she said I should rush on down because they were putting out a new shipment of ethnic makeup designed especially for African-American women—marked 50% off. When I reminded her of my Anglo-Saxon lineage, she said she really believed I could wear the lightest shade by June if I started sunbathing now.

What a sad state of the union when proud, beautiful blonde women are forced to dye their hair blue and go out into public looking like they are auditioning for a traveling minstrel show because their makeup is fourteen shades too dark. The next thing you know, American women will be forced to do what French women have always chosen to do—neglect their underarms. With God, Mrs. J and the B.B.B.B's as my witnesses, that's where I'm drawing the line at frugality.

If not for that conversation with Mrs. J., the $13.00 a week that Mike Huckabee said I'd get wouldn't sound like very much—no more than finding a handful of change under the couch cushions or a crumpled dollar in the dryer filter. Times are really tough, so $13.00 a week will go a long way toward maintaining my beauty routine. If I save up for a month, it will practically pay for a visit to the beauty salon to touch up my black roots. A month and ½ of stimulus money will keep me in Light Blue perfume by Dolce and Gabanna for six months. If I save for a mere week and ½, I can get my acrylic nails refilled and polished with my favorite color, Don't Socratease Me. Three weeks of saving will allow me to order a tube of Yves Saint Laurent concealer from Saks in NYC. Worrying about the economy has multiplied my crow's feet and deepened my frown lines. Six months of saving could pay for Botox that I need so badly. Happily, two weeks of saving will allow me to buy Mary Kay makeup in a color that matches my skin tone perfectly. And, most stimulating of all, one week of Obama money will purchase Venus razor refills and a bottle of Secret Platinum deodorant.

My only questions are, when is my first $13.00 going to reach my wallet? How will it get there; and when will I know to start spending it?

THE TOO SHORT TENNIS SKIRT SOCIETY

The other evening during a women's senior tennis match, a teammate overheard some young fellows who were waiting for a court, call us "old ladies." As we were basking in the afterglow of victory under a hut at the Sportsplex and taking our sweet time replaying every point of our victory, she broke the news of their insensitive comments.

"Who? Surely, not us. Old ladies. That's ridiculous! We are out here playing tennis. The old ladies are at home crocheting doilies." Why, out of the thousands of female residents over fifty in the Pine Belt area, which includes Laurel, Hattiesburg and Meridian, only fifty-six of them play 3.5 level tennis. Furthermore, out of those 56 athletes, the eleven women on my team are among the best in the state and will be competing for the title this May at the Sportsplex.

The comment stung like a bee. It cut like a serrated knife. It made me feel extinct. I wanted to cry. It's quite fun and dandy when we joke among ourselves about our advanced age and stage in life, but when you hear it for the first time from an outsider, it's not so amusing anymore.

My first reaction was to challenge the young whippersnapper to a single's match and show him who is old, but my hip had a catch in it. My second thought was to give him a piece of my mind, but decided there wasn't enough of it left to spare on him. Feeling deflated, I put my racquet away and took my busted bubble to the restroom where I took a candid look into a heartless mirror. The image staring back at me was not that of an old woman, but of a woman who has definitely earned her stripes. She will be old one day very soon, but not this day.

I have thought about being called an old lady frequently since that night. It troubles me that younger people consider someone my age old. What exactly constitutes "old" and will I be aware when it happens? Will I go to bed one night as a middle-aged woman and wake up the next morning with old written on my forehead?

We have all seen women of the Red Hat Society around and about. They embrace old age with verve and humor while wearing purple outfits with red hats that don't match. Inspired by the famous poem "When I am an Old Woman I Shall Wear Purple," these women have won my respect for being audacious enough to spit in the eye of old age. Personally, my family would lock me up if I went out in public in such a get up. I have decided to form a more suitable old-age society called the "Too Short Tennis Skirt Society." Perhaps the following poem will inspire old lady tennis players all over the world.

When I am an old woman, I shall wear my tennis skirts too short with breezy tops for sunning age spots. I will wear my cap backwards and squint at the sun and abandon sunscreen because the damage is done. And I shall spend my retirement on blue tennis shoes and dangling ear bobs and oversized racquets, and say I've no money for frivolous things. I shall fall down with laughter on the court when I am tired and call good shots out if I wish. I shall run my racquet along the fence when losing doesn't suit me and call you a heifer if you tick me off. I shall talk loudly at matches and throw balls asunder and not keep score and no one will protest because I am old. I will dance by myself if the music moves me. I will toot my horn at drive-thru windows when the service is slow and drive my car in the middle of the road and neighbors will know to get out of my way. I shall fetch the paper in my socks and eat from other people's plates and be content to sit and ask others to fetch and be politically incorrect if I've a mind to. I shall wear tennis shoes to the beach and not be afraid to splash in the ocean with the sharks because I am old and a little bit crazy besides. If you are fat I will tell you outright and I will eat chocolate chip cookies for supper or in the middle of the night. I shall hoard tennis balls and keep candy bars in fruit jars and never dust the furniture or clean the commode and skip polishing my toes. When I am an old woman I don't want to wear purple with a red hat that doesn't go. I'll wear tennis skirts too short because I won't believe that I am old.

COUNTRY MUSIC – THAT'S MY THANG

My very classy and good friend, Judy McCraw, and I take a lot of ridiculing from our younger friends because we like and appreciate classic country music. If we take a road trip with the young 'uns and feel the need to hear Conway, George, Delbert or Waylon, they immediately plug their ears and start singing Motley Crew or Bon Jovi songs at the top of their lungs. We are ten years older, which sometimes makes for a generation gap the size of the Grand Canyon. Although we do appreciate the music that conjures up youthful impulses in them, they have zero tolerance for ours. When they were in kindergarten learning their ABCs, we were dancing the pony to "Mony Mony" as we simultaneously learned from our daddies the words to "Hello Darlin."

My appreciation of country music goes way back to my childhood and Saturday nights listening to the Grand Ole Opry live from Nashville on our RCA stereo. It was on cold, clear nights that those distant sound waves were the clearest. My daddy would draw me onto his lap where I would snuggle against his shoulder and listen contentedly to the fiddling, the lonesome, and the somebody-done-somebody-wrong songs into the night. Because he enjoyed them, the crystalline voice of Patsy Cline, the ethereal lyrics of Hank Williams, and the unconventional sounds of Johnny Cash,s made a lasting impression on me at an early age.

During my teenage years, I strayed from my country roots for the music that was predicted to be the ruination of an entire generation. As a child of the mid-fifties, I came of age at the omega of the more innocent years of rock-n-roll and at the alpha of the raucous, rebellious years of rock music. My daughter is jealous that I experienced the Woodstock era from a safe distance and lived the music that she thinks is the best ever recorded. It's hard to say if the music was a catalyst or a by-product of the rebellious sixties, but it unquestionably defined that generation. Their mantra was to "Turn on, tune in and drop-out." Today, the music has remained timeless while the participants are sixty-plus and need Viagra to turn on, hearing aids to tune in, and Polident to keep their teeth from dropping out.

In the summer of '76, when I was with child, my husband

and I took a road trip to Nashville and the Smokey Mountains. At a truck stop outside of Nashville, we bought an eight-track tape of country music hits. Since I was pregnant and often barefoot, country music seemed the perfect fit for my stereotypical condition. Before we reached our destination, I was singing "D-I-V-O-R-C-E" along with Tammy Wynette and "Don't Come Home a'Drankin' with Loving on Your Mind" with the coal miner's daughter. The purchase of that tape sparked a new phase in our lives—Texas-two-steppin', upwardly mobile, not-so-urban cow couple.

The CMA should reserve a special place for John Travolta in the Country Music Hall of Fame for his role as Bud Davis in the movie *Urban Cowboy*. That movie single handedly brought a renaissance to the country music scene. All of a sudden, Stetsons, worn jeans, western belt buckles, and cowboy boots became haute couture. After "Looking for Love in all the Wrong Places," who would have guessed it was waiting in a honky-tonk all along?

Although we do enjoy several genres of music at our house, classic country music still rules. There are very few new country artists who live up to our standards. Most of them try too hard to be country; and their songs end up sounding like redneck nursery rhymes. The blues and country music are very similar in these respects; to sing them effectively, you have to have lived it, broken down and wallowed in the mud of despair, had your heart torn out and stomped flat, and watched the only one you ever loved walk away with your dog, truck or best friend. Until you've been there and done that, don't bellow about your International Harvester or how sexy your John Deere tractor is, because it ain't. Also, for the love of

Waylon and Willie, STOP filming videos on the beach! No matter how hard you try, you will never, ever fill Jimmy Buffett's flip-flops or Margarita glass.

Even if you don't particularly enjoy country music, you've got to admit some of the titles, lyrics and thoughts are heart rendering. Do yourself a favor, get right in your head, and really listen to Conway's "Goodbye Time," Dolly Parton's "I Will Always Love You" and "He Stopped Loving Her Today," by George "no show" Jones.

Then, if you still don't like country music, in a less offensive version of Hank Williams, Jr.'s words, "you can kiss my grits."

HAPPY BIRTHDAY, BARBIE

Believe it or not, Barbie has reached the big 5-0, the half century mark, with nary a wrinkle, varicose vein, speck of cellulite or gray hair. Barbie has survived harsh criticism for everything from being too WASPY looking (white, Anglo-Saxon and Protestant) to being too materialistic. In impressionable, young girls, she's been blamed for everything from poor self-image to eating disorders. In Iran, she's banned from entering the country, and reviled as the Satanic doll for her Western garb and lifestyle. She's been called a role model to preteens and drag queens alike, and the antithesis to the feminist movement. Barbie's perfect facial features and unrealistic body measurements immediately incensed feminists in the '60s at the height of Barbie mania. If she were human, she would be 5-foot-6, weigh about 110 pounds, wear size seven shoes and measure 39-18-33—an impossible combination of Dolly Parton, Scarlett O'Hara, and Twiggy.

Even with all the harsh criticism, it's still hard to feel sorry for Barbie. After all, time has stood for her while the rest of us have had to deal with the ravages of time and gravity. She has remained suspended in time, perpetually in her twenties, while we other female products of the 1950's have watched ourselves regress into unrecognizable images of the goddesses we once were.

Of course, Barbie evolved with the times to remain politically correct. She began showing up on the store shelves in an array of nationalities and skin colors. She took on the role of a CEO complete with executive outfits for her job and designer party clothes for the evening. Ken, the boyfriend came along in 1961. He wasn't much of a catch with his flocked hair, preppy yachtsman's outfit and effeminate looks. Ken just never gave me the impression of being a "man's man." As far as I know, Barbie never officially married Ken, but young girls all over the world unofficially united them in matrimony all the while fantasizing about their own wedding day.

Don't feel sorry for me, but I have to confess that I never owned a Barbie doll as a young girl. I preferred playing with frogs, Etch-A-Sketches and baseballs. If I had owned a Barbie doll, my boy cousins would have ridiculed me and most probably beheaded her by running over her perfectly coiffed head with a Tonka-toy bulldozer.

Now that she is half a century old, I started thinking that

maybe it's time for Barbie to grow up like the rest of us. She's lived in the lap of luxury and enjoyed shopping for designer clothes, exotic travels, a stint as Miss America and a house in Malibu. Plus, she has never gained an ounce of weight and doesn't know what a wrinkle is. She's never had to put up with a husband(s), lost her figure bearing children, driven an old hoopty car or shopped at Wal-Mart. Honestly, Barbie needs to be brought to reality; and I've come up with a couple new Barbie ideas of my own.

Change of Life Barbie: This Barbie comes wearing a "Fabulous Fifty" T-shirt, elastic-waist, stretch pants and Easy Spirit shoes. She changes her name to Barbara and tells Ken to hit the road after decades of fruitless dating. She starts dating Joe the pharmacist — a balding, pudgy man-doll sold separately that comes with a white lab coat, groomable toupee and a mortar and pestle. They met at the pharmacy where he compounds her hormone replacement therapy. She is sold complete with her monthly osteoporosis treatment, sleeping pills and a tiny, battery-operated fan for recurring hot flashes. The new Barbie is no longer 5'6" and 110 pounds. Barbara stands 5'2" and weighs 155 pounds. Her bust measurement is still 39 inches (that's in length). Her waist is now 38 inches instead of 18 and her hips have spread to a luscious 43 inches from the willowy 33 inches of her youth.

Casino Barbie: Barbie shortens her name to Barb and is sold wearing a sequined tunic top, dark denim jeans, flashy costume jewelry, metallic gold jelly sandals and a leopard print tote that she purchased at the outlet mall on the way to the casinos. Barb did marry Ken in 1965, but after forty years of marriage, he divorced her and married her younger sister, Skipper. Barb's weight ballooned after having four children, but she is back to her Malibu-Barbie weight with the aid of cigarettes, Nutri-System and the divorce proceedings. Accessories, including a portable oxygen machine, driving glasses, collagen treatments, a 1996 Cadillac, as well as her fun-loving gambling and traveling buddies—the equally realistic Teensy, Mimi, Darlene and Lola dolls, are sold separately.

I read where Mattel is throwing a big birthday bash for Barbie in an actual Malibu beach house designed by one of America's top designers.

Nobody ever said life was fair. Happy birthday, Barbie!

WHAT IS VICTORIA'S SECRET?

Yesterday, I found a paradox in my mailbox. The calendar and my mood tell me it's January, but the temperature feels more like spring, minus pink azaleas, yellow pollen and a blue sky. This typically gray, winter day has me longing for the beach, but the thought of going public in a swimsuit makes me queasy. Withdrawal symptoms from eating an estimated 6.7 dozen holiday cookies and enough bread pudding to sink a barge, are making my life miserable. My digital scales don't accuse me of a weight gain, but we all know that they lie. Rolls of dimpled, spongy fat weigh less than muscle. My thighs are the color and consistency of cottage cheese, but at least they coordinate nicely with my abdomen. The two checks I wrote to the tax collector and my credit card carrier could have paid for a total face-lift or pre-arranged my funeral. At my age, I don't know which would be the wiser investment. The stock market started dropping like the ball in Time's Square on New Year's, thus adding 5 to 10 years to my sentence in the work force. The concrete on my carport is sweating profusely—my personal predictor for tornadic activity. My washing machine ran away and flooded my house--twice, and someone backed over my husband's car. I sure could use a little good news today.

The winter doldrums--the reds, the blues, or whatever the heck this is feels like I'm wearing an itchy, wool coat or a belt that's too tight. I desperately need to shed them and run barefoot through the sand on a deserted island so no one has to witness the sight of me in a swimsuit.

To top off this dreary day, the mailman delivered a disheartening copy of Victoria's Secret 2008 swimsuit catalog along with a highly informative edition of the AARP Bulletin. Holding one in each hand, I couldn't help but laugh at the irony of it. Just as it was when I was fourteen, my current age can be described as "between." Back then, I was too old for dolls, but not old enough to date. Today, I'm too old for Brazilian bikinis, but not old enough for Medicare.

I sat down at the kitchen table and placed the publications side by side and alternately turned the pages of one and then the other. Victoria told me the style for 2008 calls for "Less is more, as long as it's high-shine, high-glamour and worn with high, high heels. The suits are standout chic that shimmers beachside, magnetizes poolside and turns every side into your best side." My bunion throbbed, and I gagged a little at the thought of it.

AARP made a pathetic attempt at excitement with, "Watch out America! Here comes the 50 plus election!" Whoop-de-do. A scientific poll on the adjoining page then shamed me with the fact that 30% of people my age have already pre-arranged their funerals. There goes my face-lift.

So, I turned a few more pages in search of anything that might apply to my "tweener" status. The choices were brutal on every page. I could choose to reverse my tops and bottoms, switch 'em. Flip 'em. Two is always more fun than one, or I could opt to make my house work for me by obtaining a reverse mortgage. The last thing I need is a reversible, snakeskin, brass-ringed-bikini. Frankly, what I need is for gravity and time to reverse, not my stupid mortgage. I pressed onward.

The choices were fabulously inapplicable. Catalog left offered, "New! Removable padding for coverage just where you need it." Magazine right inquired, "Do you have diabetes? Are you on Medicare? If you answered yes to both questions, the cost of your diabetes testing supplies may be covered." My answers were--I need all the padding "up there" that I can get. I have been eating a lot of sweets lately, and NO! Why is everybody so concerned about my coverage?

Then, on page 30 of the AARP Bulletin I spied an ad that tore the paradox asunder. This is exactly what it said: "Erectile dysfunction is routinely covered by Medicare." They must be kidding me. Doesn't Medicare have more pressing health problems to cover? If Medicare routinely covers E.D., then why shouldn't it cover equally perky enhancements of the female form? At my age, there wasn't an article or advertisement in their entire bulletin that addressed a single one of my needs. Then and there I decided to cancel my membership in the A.A.R.P. They can keep their propaganda, senior discounts and helpful information out of my mailbox.

As for Victoria? She has a secret, and I'm still plenty young enough to want to know what it is. She can keep those catalogs coming.

MAMMOGRAMS –
A SOLUTION TO TERRORISM

It was the hottest day recorded so far this year and the worst day possible to be sans deodorant. Before I stepped out of my car onto the surface of the sun, I sprayed my underarms with a fourth dose of Heavenly angel mist then wondered aloud in the parking lot how French women can stand to live with themselves without deodorant. A man walking by thought I was trying to make conversation with him. I just smiled apologetically and made my way, holding my arms ballerina-like away from my torso, into the cool of the building.

The receptionist directed me down the hall, to the right,

first door on the left. It had been five years since my last visit there. My disregard for that part of my anatomy was as dangerous as driving at night without headlights. It's just human nature to put off doing things that aren't all that pleasant.

Three other women were waiting, and we were soon joined by two more. One woman was well put together and a bit younger than me. Another was about my age, dressed neatly casual and was accompanied by her mother. The two other women were older, one Caucasian and one African-American. The pragmatist that I am, the research I had done online had me weighing the odds. Out of the six women in the waiting room, there was a great probability that one of us already had or in the future would be diagnosed with breast cancer. As it normally does in stressful situations and always in hospital waiting rooms, my heart suddenly skipped a beat at the possibility. Would the unfortunate verdict be awarded to me or to the chatty woman who had just told everyone about her grandchildren? Or would it be the quiet African-American lady reading a book she brought from home? Although I had never met any of the women waiting that day, I hoped that no one in our cross-section of American women would ever have to use the "C" word when referring to themselves.

Shortly, a slender woman emerged from the testing area just as another lady entered the waiting room. The two women immediately recognized each other and embraced. It was apparent that the women were members of the sisterhood of the survivors of breast cancer. Although my heart ached for them, I also felt a sense of selfish relief. Their mere presence in that room had just decreased my odds greatly. Out of the eight of us present, statistics said that only one was predicted to develop breast cancer; but there were TWO. Maybe, I was off the hook.

If you have ever had a mammogram, you know what happened next.

Is this routine? *Yes*. Five years since your last mammogram? *Yes*. The technician gave me a scolding sideways glance. Do you have implants? *Surely, she jests*. Age at first pregnancy? *21*. Are you on HRT? *Yes, for three years*. Relatives who had breast cancer still the same? *Yes*. *One aunt and one great-aunt had breast cancer*. Did you wear deodorant today? *How professional of her to pretend she didn't notice.*

If water boarding is considered inhumane treatment for the prisoners at Gitmo, I have a simple solution. Why don't the interrogators implement male mammograms as a means of interrogation? Thousands of women on a daily basis willingly surrender themselves to this form of torture in the name of preventive health care. I suspect the government could find out the whereabouts of Osama bin Laden and the location and intent of terrorist cells worldwide if they would simply "clamp down" on certain tender parts of the detainees with cold hard plastic. This long terrorist nightmare might be over in a matter of days. We could pull our troops out of Iraq and Afghanistan, save billions of dollars on national defense, and bring about world peace with one machine and a motivated mammographer, preferably someone who has lost a loved one at the hands of terrorists.

Yesterday, I found the promised results letter from my

OB-GYN in the mailbox. Fear caused a rush of adrenaline to shoot down my arms causing my fingers to shiver. Was my life about to be forever changed in the middle of the driveway? As I breathlessly scanned the letter, the words "happy to inform you" jumped off the page. I felt like I had won a trip to Disney World.

Seriously, my mammogram was not that uncomfortable and well worth the peace of mind it brought. If you are procrastinating about having one as I did, call your doctor's office and have them set it up. The procedure just might save your life, and in the hands of the right persons, could squash terrorism flat in its tracks.

Part 5:

MY GREATEST

gifts

A MAN AND TWO TRUCKS

The biggest fan of my columns (you know who you are and I adore you) inquired of my daughter as to why I never write specifically about my son. It is easy to write about my daughter because she still lives under my roof and is marginally under my jurisdiction. Clark is a married man and hasn't been under my thumb for several years. He will always remain my blue-eyed man-child with a killer sense of humor who just so happens to be the best looking man to come along since Brad Pitt, honestly. We share a love for Jimmy Buffett, the beach, tennis shoes and cars. We have the same skin, the same smile, and the same worried crease between our brows. He can belt out an Elvis or Johnny Cash tune at will and has some stage-worthy impersonations—Rocky, every character from *Jaws*, Billy Bob Thornton in

Slingblade, and even his own father. When I look into his eyes, I see so much of myself that it scares me to death at times. When he was a toddler, I could have eaten him alive because he was such a perfectly sweet child. In his college days, I wished that gypsies had stolen him from his crib.

When he walked into our back door last Saturday and placed the keys to his truck on the counter, it was an affirmation that he had finally come full circle.

"Mom, these keys have been in my pocket through some tough stuff over the last six years. It's sad to see it go. I listened to a little Buffett on the way over here. It almost made me cry." I understood exactly what he was talking about. Let me start this from the beginning.

In 1985, Phil's dad bought a brown and white Silverado with all the bells and whistles. He had a habit of driving with his left hand while he relaxed his right arm across the top of the seat. After he passed away in 2001, sixteen years of gardening, sweat and toil were evident as the exact imprint of his hand was embedded into the leather. In 2002 we took possession of the brown truck, and Clark nicknamed it Old Blue. It made perfect sense to him. He parked his high octane Mustang GT and shined up the old warhorse like a new penny, taking special care not to disturb the imprint of his grandfather's hand. It served as an inspiration to him as he drove back and forth to William Carey College to finish his degree in biology. That handprint was a pat on the back every time he successfully aced a test or passed a class with flying colors. He took more than a few wrong turns during his early college days, but an inner strength that borders on divine intervention put him on the right path at the right time.

His grandfather succumbed to Lou Gehrig's disease and wasn't there to see him graduate from William Carey, but he had definitely been riding with him in that Silverado. When he was accepted to attend the University of St. Augustine School of Physical Therapy, we gave him our 1998 Ford F-150 because it was more practical for a married man who was about to embark on the most pivotal journey of his life.

And drive it he and his young bride did. For over four years, mostly on holidays and always late at night, we would anxiously listen for the familiar hum of the F-150 engine as it pulled wearily up our driveway. In 2004, he made an unscheduled flying trip home for my father's funeral. When he walked in the back door, I was reminded that a part of my daddy was still alive in him.

Six hundred miles each way is a long haul when home is the only place you want to be. Jimmy Buffett songs—*The Far Side of the World* collection in particular — were his mantra and inspiration. His and Amanda's visits were never long enough, but he always left us with this knowledge, "I've got business on the East Coast to take care of." No matter how hard I tried to hold them back, tears leaked out every time he hesitantly departed our driveway and turned south into the future.

Americans have always had a love affair with their cars. That love affair is even more evident in our family since we've owned no less than two dozen over the past thirty-something years. Some cars are easy to let go, but others become a part of the family story like Old Blue and the 1998 F-150.

We bought the F-150 in 1998 not knowing all the places it would go. Last Saturday, we bought it back again because we knew precisely where it had been and exactly how tough Clark's journey to the far side of the world was. There was no way we could let that epic journey park anywhere but here where it all started.

THE "LOVE TO COOK" GENE

Apparently, the love of cooking is an inherited condition. To my knowledge, science has not delved into it since the love of cooking is not a disease that threatens mankind. The love of cooking can contribute to obesity, which does pose a huge health problem, but the two don't necessarily coexist in the same individual.

Somewhere in the nucleus of each cell in every human being is a tiny chromosome, and in that chromosome is a gene that determines if a person will love to cook or will just do it to keep from starving. I imagine the LTC (love to cook) gene will be found in conjunction with the patience and creativity genes. At first glance, the three genes will look very similar in composition, but closer magnification should reveal that the LTC gene is in the shape of a teeny-weenie, itty-bitty, iron skillet.

Furthermore, the LTC gene won't be found exclusively in the female species. For instance, a mother can pass it on to her son, where it lies unused for thirty-two years. That son then passes it on to his only daughter where it becomes so dominant that it trumps the puny keep from starving gene that was inherited from the mother of the child.

This theory came to me the other night while I lay in bed thinking about my daughter and how she has some amazing qualities that I don't possess—the LTC gene in particular. She came home from summer classes at Ole Miss to celebrate Father's Day with us. She reminds me of bubbles blown out of a wand, the way she comes floating in and out of our lives. She is effervescent, sparkling, unpredictable and so full of life that she may pop at any second. She floated through the back door and piled all her belongings on the kitchen's island countertop, the distribution point for all things that enter or exit here. After a long spell of hugging, she broke away from me and went straight to my cookbook nook. She pulled out *The Mississippi Cookbook*, a favorite one that my husband gave to me for my first Valentine's Day as a married woman. It has served me well and in my hour of need made it appear that deep in my molecular makeup lurks the LTC gene. She went straight to the pie section, frantically flipping pages in search of something, "Oh my gosh, here it is! The caramel pie that Mrs. Sybil made for the church bake sale. It sold for $100. I've got to make this for Daddy. He will absolutely love it!"

When my daughter was about three years old, Santa Claus brought her a miniature stove complete with tiny pots, pans, utensils, dishes and plastic food that she happily pretended to cook and serve to us. "Happily" being the operative word here. Just like her grandmother Ouida and her mother before her, cooking for the people she loves makes her happy. I have been muddling my way around the kitchen for thirty-something years impersonating women that love to cook when in reality I've done it just to keep my loved ones from starving. There is a huge difference between the two, and that's where the genetic link comes in. They have the "gene" that passed me by.

For two hours last night, my oft-abandoned kitchen was alive with the ringing of pots, the whir of the mixer, and spoons making sweet music against glass mixing bowls. She looked at it as an adventure as she moved through each step of the recipe with the adeptness of Paula Deen. I kept thinking that Cool Whip and Jello pudding mix would have been the way to go. It took both of us working feverishly over two eyes of the stove to bring the caramel, filling and meringue to a crescendo at just the right moment. At one point she confessed, "No wonder that pie went for a hundred dollars. This is awesome! You need four hands and four feet all at once to cook it!"

After the flour dust had settled, and every kitchen implement and vessel imaginable was in the sink, the pie that we pulled from the oven was almost too pretty to eat. She admired the golden peaks of the meringue from several angles as it sat cooling on the stovetop. "I can't wait to take Mammaw a piece of it. I hope Dad likes it!" She was glowing. I was wilting like week-old lettuce. I don't have it and certainly don't understand it, but that LTC gene surely is a marvelous and mysterious thing to behold.

HERE COMES THE BRIDE

Most other women with access to blabbing in a weekly newspaper would have announced to the world that she had become a MOB (mother of the bride) the moment it happened. I officially became a MOB on September 21, 2007. My delay in writing about my new title is not because I am not absolutely thrilled to pieces. My tardiness is due to the fact that I couldn't decide which angle to take. My first inclination was to write a sentimental column about how time is a sneaky thief that steals your collagen and snatches baby girls from your arms. One morning you are swaddling your BTB (bride-to-be) in a yellow blanket, and just like that, she's six years old, skipping down the driveway to board a school bus with a Barney backpack into which she has secretly stuffed that same yellow blanket. Don't blink, because if you do, the next thing you know, you will be pulling a U-Haul of precious cargo off to college. You will be stoic when you drive away with a full heart and an empty U-Haul because she is so ready to spread her wings and fly; and you have to let her. Trust me, the tears will come about five miles down the road, and her father will pat your hand in silence because the lump in his throat is so big he can't say a word. Within a half a blink, a 6 foot 5 son of a preacher man, the kind of man you prayed God would send, asks for her hand in marriage. But, (sniff, sniff) I am not going to do that.

Although I'm not one of them, some mothers start planning their daughter's wedding even before they are born. At this point, my experience as a MOB can be classified as ain't got a clue what to do. Five years ago when my son got married, acronyms for the wedding party weren't in fashion like they are today. I was a MOG (mother of the groom) and didn't even know it. My former MOB friends inform me that my new exalted position will basically consume my life for the next year. I have also been told that the FOB's only role is to pay up, shut up and smile blankly when he walks his daughter down the aisle. Our own FOB in the upcoming wedding has already offered to write the FUG (future groom) a low-ball, five-figure check, no strings attached, if he will whisk our lovely daughter to the JOP (Justice of the Peace) for their nuptials. The FOB has also offered to have the grill hot and ready for a wedding barbecue upon their return from the JOP.

The BTB burst into tears at such a tacky and insensitive proposition from the FOB. She says the wedding will be highly liturgical, held in the candlelight, with none other than the FOG (father of the groom) donning his robe and stole to perform the ceremony. The BTB says the gown will be haute couture and designed by Monique Lhuillier. Let's just say, you can't buy it out of the J.C. Penney catalog, and the price tag is a tad bit less than the bribery check the FOB offered to write the FUG.

The MOG (mother of the groom) and I are to wear gowns that are similar but the colors must not clash and one can't upstage the other. Some BTB must deal with the sticky situation of what role the SMOB (stepmother of the bride) and the SMOG (stepmother of the groom) play in the wedding. Thankfully, this does not apply to our family, as I am positive there would be a clash (and I don't mean gown color) between the MOB and the SMOB if she tried to steal my thunder. There will be several bridesmaids comprised of GOB (girlfriends of the bride), a SLOB (sister-in-law of the bride), a COB (cousin of the bride) in addition to PG (punch girls), and RAT (registry attendants).

The groom's party will be made up of a variety of dashing gentlemen—most prominently the BM (best man) and a matching number of GM (groomsmen), plus ushers who are BOG (brothers of the groom), FOG (friends of the groom) and a BOB (brother of the bride). Unfortunately, there will be no SOB or SOG (sisters of the bride or groom) because none were born to either PAC (parents of the couple). The flower girl position may be up for grabs because the NOG (niece of the groom) will just be toddling around by then, and you never know what havoc a toddler might wreak on the ceremony.

I'm definitely without compass over this MOB stuff, but I

do have an idea of the general direction we are headed since pouring over the latest edition of Inside Weddings. The BTB's "something old" should definitely be a tiny piece of the yellow blanket. Her "something new" will be the Monique Lhuiller gown. Something borrowed will be the money to pay for it all, and "something blue" will be the FOB when I hand him the final bill. I will smile sweetly and remind him, "You always said you would do anything for da baby dirl."

THE LELLOW BLANKIE

On a recent trip to the beach, I had the pleasure of sharing a luscious
king-sized bed with my daughter while the men folk were forced to
sleep wherever they could lay their heads. She and I are very picky
about our sleeping arrangements and can't fathom how men can
fall asleep anywhere that they come to a stop. While renovating the
condo after Hurricane Ivan, my husband once slept on the tile floor
with nothing but a rolled-up drop cloth for a pillow. I would have
required admittance to a hospital after a night on a cold, hard floor,
but he was well rested and chipper that he had saved $100 on a hotel
room.

When she was a baby and sick, the only place she could find

rest was on top of me with her legs draped over my thighs and her feverish head resting in the hollow of my neck. She went through different phases where she would not go to sleep without one or more of her chosen stuffed animals. One week her bedfellow might be a Ninja Turtle and the next a hairy monkey or a rubber Gumby. For several years, her favorite was a tiny stuffed chicken no bigger than the palm of my hand. We lost and found that stupid chicken in motel rooms across the southeast. She finally abandoned it when its feathers began to look like they had been rolled in tar. For months, she even slept with a battery-operated Mickey Mouse toothbrush. The switch on the toothbrush was trigger happy, and I awoke startled many a night to the tune of Mickey chirping "Brush, brush, brush your teeth each and every day!"

Although her strange bedfellows have changed innumerable times over the years, and in four months will be replaced by a brawny bearded man who snores at a decibel level matched only by her father, one companion in her bed has remained constant—her "lellow blankie."

The color scheme for her nursery was yellow, and I was showered with all things yellow before her arrival. We brought her home from the hospital in a white Feltman Brothers dress and wrapped her in a yellow, satin-trimmed blanket. Like her brother before her, she quickly learned to suck her thumb while rubbing the satin trim of the blanket between her long, artistic fingers. Her poor brother lost his blanket on a trip to Disney World when he was three. He mourned the loss of his blanket for only a few days and eventually gave up thumb-sucking cold turkey because one without the other just didn't satisfy his craving.

That night at the beach as we turned down the comforter, she plopped her pillow from home onto the head of the bed. Inside her pillowcase was that old familiar lumpiness of her most prized possession—her "lellow blankie."

I quipped, "Thought you stopped dragging that dingy thing everywhere since you got engaged." She answered very seriously, "Are you kidding me? This blanket's going with me on my honeymoon. The only place I didn't take it was to England when I went with the JC choir. I just couldn't risk taking it that far away from home. It's been with me through two colleges, four apartments, Myrtle Beach, L.A, Las Vegas, Memphis, Iuka, Branson, Chicago, New York, San Antonio, San Francisco, Vail, St. Augustine and a hundred trips to the beach. Do you remember when I almost lost it on that horrible sixth-grade trip to Washington, D.C.?"

"How could I ever forget that nightmare? We thought we had lost you too, but you were in the basement laundry of our hotel looking for it. By gosh, you weren't leaving there without it. I'll never forget the triumphant look on your face when you stepped out of that elevator with "lellow blankie" in your arms again."

Her sweet green eyes verged on tears, "Mama, that was awful! All the girls made fun of me and wouldn't let me sit with them on the way home."

"What do you think they would say now if they knew you are still sleeping with it and plan to take it on your honeymoon?"

"You know, I don't care what they think about me now, but I sure did back then."

Just before we drifted off to sleep, I asked exactly when was the last time she washed "lellow blankie." She told me that she couldn't recall but that it had probably been a couple of years because it is in such fragile condition these days. Then she mumbled sleepily that she might wash it after her honeymoon to New York in November.

Until then she wants it to smell the same as it always has... like love, home, far- away places, comfort, sweet dreams and the inimitable perfume of her twenty-three years of life.

WAITING FOR A VERY SPECIAL PACKAGE

My recently betrothed daughter came bouncing down the stairs Tuesday morning and announced in a tone of voice that might indicate Elvis had just been spotted alive in Arkansas, "This is the day they are shipping it! I'm so excited I can't stand it! It's been five whole months!"

She has always adored receiving things by mail, UPS or Fed Ex. A creative, thoughtful and solitary child, she spent untold hours reading *Goosebumps* mystery books and pouring over Disney catalogs. Her world was one of whimsy, bubble baths, paint by number and secret melodies. From the beginning, she marched to the beat of a drum that most people couldn't begin to hear.

With pre-adolescence, she turned her attention from Disney

characters toward surfer-girl clothing, a blue guitar and J. Peterman catalogs. Those were the romantic *Titanic* years. After watching the movie thirteen times at the theatre, she became obsessed with anything *Titanic*. Naturally, she found a semi-precious reproduction of the Heart of the Ocean necklace in a catalog and begged me to order it so she could wear it in a talent show. The day it came in the mail, she was glowing as she put it on with a vintage dress we found at the Salvation Army. As she sat down at the piano and began to sing and play the love theme from the movie, I was comforted with the feeling that I must be doing something right. I knew that moment was one of pure perfection and love that might never visit me again. I was wrong.

Last November, when we and three of her bridesmaids trekked from Oxford to Brinkley, Arkansas, to shop for a wedding gown, the car was full of magazines, wedding day wishes and unbridled anticipation. We had heard about Low's Bridal from several sources and just wanted to see for ourselves what all the hoopla was about

Since we were a little late for our 1 o'clock appointment, we went straight to the task of looking for "the dress" among the thousands on mannequins and in racks. By 4 o'clock, our bridal consultant was ready to throw in the towel, and the BTB was prepared to give up the fight. Exquisite visions of white lace, beads and crystals lay strewn across the floor, cast aside for not being "the one." Our BC summoned the shop's owner as a Hail Mary effort to send the despondent BTB across the wedding gown goal line. The BTB showed her the picture of the elusive inspiration dress. "Hmmm. I see where you are going. A dress very similar to this just arrived this morning. We haven't even priced it yet. Let's give it a try!"

The wilted BTB suddenly perked up when she laid her eyes on the illusion the BC draped before her. Of the dozens of dresses she had tried on, none of them gave her the look she had in her eyes now.

"Hurry, hurry, try it on," her BM were clapping and jumping up and down in place."

All the time I'm privately panicking, "This is "the dress" and we don't know how much it costs. Will it reside on the break-the-bank third floor, the home-equity-loan second floor, or the we-can-totally-handle-that first floor"?

When she stepped out of the dressing room, her green eyes were sparkling and brimming with tears, "Oh, mama, this is it, (let's pause and get a Kleenex because I'm crying as I write this) but what if it costs too much?"

It was the moment that all mothers dream about sharing with their daughters. It was the moment that nullified ten hours of labor, and countless sleepless nights and gave meaning to every sacrifice, every heartache, and every doubt I ever had about the rewards of motherhood.

My mind flashed back to the days of Disney catalogs, Barney the purple dinosaur and the Heart of the Ocean necklace. Just like the day that she put on that necklace and played the piano and sang for me, it was one of pure perfection and love.

You guessed it. The dress was a bit out of our budget. Of course I pulled her aside and whispered, "I know this is 'the dress' because you have never looked so beautiful and radiant. I really had expected to pay this much. We'll just keep this our little secret."

This week my daughter isn't waiting impatiently for the mailman to deliver Pongo or Barney. She is waiting for UPS to deliver the most important package of her life—her wedding dress. For a little girl who always loved receiving packages and a mother who always tried to fulfill wishes, it just doesn't get any better than this.

A CLOSET FULL OF SHOES

Warning: If you are pregnant, may become pregnant or have ever been pregnant, reading this column may cause red eyes and sniffling.

I have no idea what possessed me to open that shoe closet door last Sunday morning. It seems that I am being blindsided by emotion at every turn. Barrettes, bows, baby teeth, baubles and even bubble bath bottles have joined forces to turn this MOB into a sentimental pack rat. They beg me to let them stay, but the denesting instinct tells me I must let them go.

There is no scientific proof, but expectant mothers develop an intense nesting instinct right before their babies are born. It happened to me the day before I went into labor with my son. Somewhere deep in those mysterious places of the female brain that no male possesses, a tiny unmistakable signal is sent to the womb that it is time for the life inside us to come into the world. If there is a disconnect somewhere between the two, the brain sends a warning signal for us to scrub, paint, and organize all things in our path. On February 9, 1977, a little voice told me to take a toothbrush and Comet to the tile and grout of my New-Orleans blue bathroom. When my husband returned home from work, he found me still wearing a nightgown, down on my hands and knees, wild-eyed and sway-backed, with my belly practically dragging across the blue floor. The next day, the real signal to deliver reached its intended destination. I became a mother; and the course for the rest of my life was set.

Honestly, I also believe that when mothers are faced with the reality that the same nest they built for their young is about to become empty, the brain sends an equally powerful "denesting" signal. I'm sure this isn't a Webster's approved word, but it is the only fitting one that comes to mind. Since the receptors associated with birth are now defunct or non-existent, the signal goes straight to our hearts. Therein lies the problem.

There is no other way to explain why a closet full of abandoned shoes brought me to tears.

There they were, all twenty-three pair, thrown helter-skelter, more or less in chronological order of their last wearing. Ohhh...the pink Dalmatian goulashes made a big splash in New York City her junior year at Ole Miss. Stylish women on Fifth Avenue inquired where they could buy a pair. "Pay Less in Oxford, Mississippi," she answered in an accent thick as day-old grits...There were those hideous Dr. Marten combat boots that cost me a small fortune. "Everybody" was wearing them she claimed, and they looked so radical with her surplus store military jacket. And, the Rocket Dog Mary Janes were just the right look to wear with that long wrap skirt the first day of high school. But, there was only one of them. I pondered a few seconds on what might have happened to its mate.

Rubber flip-flops in a sunset of colors... Does this closet belong to Jimmy Buffett? Seven pair--each pancake thin, embossed in gray by her toes and heels and still bearing sand from seashores far and near...The brown Birkenstock mules she just had to have for her high-school graduation trip to San Francisco. Neither her feet nor the Birkenstocks touched the ground as she floated like flower petals in the wind along Haight-Ashbury, high on nothing but life and the air of the city where hippydom began... Pink and blue suede New Balance sneakers laced with skull and cross-bone shoestrings. She declared the skulls weren't sinister and assured me she wasn't going to gun down her peers with a shotgun. They were purely her generation's answer to my generation's smiley face. Just one of those things that makes a mother say "hmmm..." Leather, embossed clogs she wore in the talent show that year she strummed her blue guitar so passionately that her fingers bled. To the dismay of her groupies, she came in a disappointing second to a country music act. Those silly judges just couldn't appreciate the Barenaked Ladies... And, finally the Adidas cleats, permanently cast like baby shoes in the muddy grass of high school soccer fields—trophies from an honorably mentioned career.

Each of those pairs of shoes represented a vignette of her journey with each step leading her closer and closer to this most momentous day. With her approval and the resolve provided by the denesting instinct, I actually threw about half of them in the trash and never looked back. Well...maybe once. In a little over a week, she will step into the future wearing a pair of Carrie Bradshaw-inspired, Tiffany blue wedding shoes. You read it right. I never expected the most important shoes of her life to be anything less than extraordinary.

DEERLY BELOVED

After finally getting a ring, if your precious baby daughter comes to you the way little girls do when they really want something and says she wants to have her a destination wedding, protect your sanity and your pocketbook and just say NO. If her begging eyes well up with tears and her bottom lip begins to tremble and pooch, turn your back and say absolutely NOT. If she runs to her room and slams the door behind her, don't follow her. Don't even look at her while she is in this highly emotional state because one look at the wrong time will melt your heart. If her persistence wears down your steely resolve, please take the advice of this former MOB and say NO to a destination wedding and insist upon a wedding and reception in the comfort of your own home.

Now that I have been there, done that and had a nervous breakdown to prove it, it makes perfect sense. Instead of moving all your earthly possessions to the wedding, move the wedding to your earthly possessions. If she rebuts by saying she wants to exchange her vows in a church, build a chapel in your backyard. It will be cheaper. If she says there would be no parking for all the guests, hire a fleet of limousines to shuttle the guests to and fro. It will save you money. If she says the grounds have no charm or beauty, hire a landscaper, dig a lake and build a mountain beside it with the dirt. It might not save you any money, but at least you will have a place to catch fish when it's over. If she wants to honeymoon in New York City during a subway terror alert, for her and the groom's safety, tell her she can honeymoon at home. Then pack your own bags and depart straightway under cover of darkness to a secret destination. Go alone without the father of the bride for he will be too depressed over losing his little girl and his life's savings to be any fun whatsoever. Don't come back until the last thank you note has been written. Pack lots of clothes because that could take up to a year. Other than elopement, this seems to be the perfect wedding scenario.

Currently, the only proof I have that a wedding took place is a wilted bouquet, a soiled wedding dress and a banged up car in the carport. There are some pictures taken by attendees, but MOB amnesia prevents me from recalling any of the events captured on camera. It looks like me in the pictures, but as far as I am concerned that woman is an imposter. I wasn't there, and the wedding never happened. Oh my! Someone has kidnapped my daughter because she did not come downstairs this morning, and most of her things are still here. The wedding dress is still hanging in the exact spot it has been for the past six months. The veil is still sitting atop my wardrobe on a wig mannequin. It seems I have awakened, startled by the haunting veiled head, every morning for the past year. The birdcage netting has never moved from that spot, but yet the pictures tell another story.

Before my husband left for work this morning in his quest to recoup his losses, he reminded me that I have to take the Honda to the body shop to be repaired now that the lovebirds have returned it to us. Ohhh, it's all coming back to me now — the deer that attacked the newlyweds' car on the way to the airport...the chapel in Oxford...the cold beautiful sky...the bagpipes...Holy Communion... friends and family...a rose and hydrangea bouquet...throwing autumn leaves...an emotional groom...the most beautiful bride these eyes have ever seen...who gives this woman?

I'm not sure, but they tell me her father and I did.

THE GREATEST GIFTS OF ALL

In years past, when my children were little, the tree didn't go up at our house until after Kiwanis Pancake Day and the Christmas parade. In recent years, no sooner than the Thanksgiving turkey is cleared from the table, our home becomes a flurry of golden ribbons, garlands, Santa Clauses and irreplaceable ornaments. Since becoming an adult, my recently betrothed daughter has developed a severe case of Christmas tree sentimentality. She has forbidden me to decorate it without her supervision, and hers are the only hands allowed to hang the baby's first Christmas ornament from 1985 and the tiny *Teddy Bear's Christmas* book, so old now that its origin is a mystery to us all. She made me promise that I would never decorate the tree without her. Then I reminded her that next Christmas she will be a married woman and could decorate an equally beautiful tree of her very own. Tears came to her eyes when she said, "That doesn't matter. This will always be my home and these ornaments are the story of our family. They remind me of when I was little and of that red-flannel nightgown and of one Christmas Eve when we found Santa's boot prints in the fireplace ashes. We looked outside and he had left a trampoline in the back yard that wasn't there when we went to Mammaw's. How did you and Daddy do that anyway? Remember how we'd listen to Elvis and Aaron Neville's *Soulful Christmas* while we decorated the tree? Then we'd turn on the tree lights and the candles and run through the yard and not look until we reached the middle of the road. Mama, it was always so wonderful and beautiful! Please, let's never stop doing that together..."

Her special memories made me grateful for the Christmases of my childhood. Over a half-century of them have come and gone, and with the passing of years, they enter my consciousness this time of year in twinkles and brief flashes of warmth and love.

My earliest memories are of a sugar plum tree on the sewing cabinet at my Grandmother Clark's house, of candy orange slices in a crystal bowl, and of hanging vintage glass ornaments on the flimsy limbs of a fresh-cut cedar tree. Love is all around me. There are golden ones where I am riding in a wooden trailer being pulled my grandfather's tractor. We are on a mission to find the perfect Christmas tree. My knit cap is red and my nose is too, like Rudolph's. I smell fireplaces burning wood and the sweetness of apple in the smoke trailing from his pipe as we putter along fencerows and the familiar paths of our native woods. There is a fleeting one where my daddy's hand is safely guiding mine, and we are making beautiful swirling light in the cold night with a sparkler.

Then there are pre-adolescent flashbacks to Black Cat

firecrackers, Roman candles and bottle rockets. My cousin Randy was notorious for his bad luck with fireworks and could have been the poster child for the consequences of using them without adult supervision. We are impatiently waiting for G.I. Joe, Barbie and Ken to arrive in Santa's sleigh. Somebody yells, "War!" Cousin Randy takes a Roman candle blast to his chest that sets off a pack of Black Cats in his shirt pocket. I am among the lesser wounded.

I can't recall the year we stopped hunting Christmas trees in the woods around Clark Hill. It was probably about the same time that aluminum trees illuminated by revolving kaleidoscope spotlights came into vogue. Even now, when the leaves start turning, I always catch myself scanning fencerows for the perfect tree. I haven't eaten a candy orange slice in decades. Without a grandmother's hugs, they just don't taste the same. I still love sparklers and buy myself a box of them every Christmas at the fireworks stand. Mercifully, the fireworks wars ended without tragedy — a minor miracle that we survived to adulthood with our fingers and eyes intact. We cousins like to laugh and reminisce about those Christmas Eves when all was right with the world.

I made that promise to my daughter, although my heart knows that she will be the one who breaks it. The old memories will always be a part of who she is, but they will gradually fade and be replaced by special moments that she is yet to experience. Christmas isn't about tangible things, and I'm deeply proud she has crossed the threshold that leads to this essential truth. Christmas is about the intangible gifts of tradition, love, family and faith in the One whose birthday we celebrate; for they are the greatest gifts of all.

Part 6:

LIVING

the life

THE RASBERRY RULE

After many years of battling them, I have decided that inanimate objects can be classified into three major categories—those that don't work, those that break down and those that get lost.

It is an experience common to all men to find out that everything that can go wrong will go wrong and at the worst possible moment. Whether we must attribute this to the malignity of matter or the total depravity of inanimate things, the fact holds true. (Wikapedia) This is known as Murphy's Law. At my residence, we call it the Rasberry Rule.

My reservoir of experience with objects that break down is

deep and wide, though my expertise lies with the automobile, the lawn mower and boats. With the cunning typical of its breed, the automobile never breaks down next to a repair shop full of idle mechanics. It waits until it reaches a bustling intersection in the middle of the lunch hour.

Thus it creates maximum misery, inconvenience, frustration and irritability among its human cargo, thereby raising its owner's heart rate to life-shortening levels. My daddy always referred to this unhappy human condition as being "chapped."

The thing about lawn mowers is that they are confined to a yard, so it is a given where they will break down. However, it is amazing the lengths a lawn mower will go to in order to inject the element of surprise. Brakes will suddenly fail when descending steep embankments. Belts and blades will disengage and propel themselves through the air like UFOs. Small fires will break out near the gas tank. Their bag of tricks is endless and frightening. I've never met a lawn mower that I didn't despise or whose hatred for me was not returned ten fold.

Boats, however, are a breed to themselves. Unlike cars and lawn mowers, they are not utilitarian but recreational. Humans relish their rare recreational time thus placing great pressure on inanimate objects purchased for the sole purpose of having fun. Either before it begins or at the precise moment the fun reaches a climax and all seems to be right with the world, the boat will sputter and spew then leave you up the creek, down the river or marooned at sea, drifting aimlessly without a paddle and no other humans in sight. Although the boat will be as relaxed as a frog on a lily pad, human blood pressure readings can reach stroke-inducing levels.

Washing machines, air-conditioners, computers, copiers, printers, fax machines, televisions, cell phones, refrigerators—are all in the same league with the automobile to take their turn at breaking down whenever life threatens to flow smoothly for their human counterparts.

Many inanimate objects find it extremely difficult to break down. Hammers, scissors, pliers and keys are practically incapable of breaking down. Therefore, they have had to devise a different technique for torturing man. They simply disappear.

Man has not solved the mystery of how they do it as no man has ever caught one in the act of getting lost. My theory is that they use humans as a means of locomotion while inflicting temporary amnesia. We facilitate their disappearance then later have absolutely no recollection of how, when or where we put them. Husbands accuse wives, wives accuse children and children implicate pets. Happy the household is in turmoil, the lost object sits smugly in the exact spot you left it the last time you used it.

I am fascinated by the fact that things that break down virtually never get lost and vice-versa. An air-conditioner will invariably break down at the height of a summer heat wave, but it will never get lost. My glasses, which have the potential to break down, hardly ever do. They prefer to drive me crazy by running away several times a day.

Now to the third class of objects—those that don't work—is the most baffling of all. These include such objects as battery-powered radios, cigarette lighters, flashlights and gift clocks. It is inaccurate to say that they never work. They work initially, and then quit for no good reason. In fact, it is widely accepted that they are built for the purpose of not working. Some people have reached old age without ever seeing some of these objects—flashlights, for example—in working order.

They have truly defeated man by conditioning him never to expect anything of them, and in return they have given us the only peace we receive from inanimate society. We do not expect a radio to work during a tornado warning, a flashlight to work after the unheeded tornado downs power lines, or a lighter to work when we need to light a candle because the flashlight didn't work. We simply attribute it to Murphy's Law, or in my case—the Rasberry Rule—and go placidly, pulse: 72, BP: 120/80, about our humanly business.

PHOBIAS AT 40,000 FEET

It's about that time of year when families begin planning their vacations. Just last night, I asked Phil when he was going to take his vacation and what destination he had in mind. As usual, our conversation ended in a tiff. You see, since September 11, 2001, he has refused to fly anywhere under any condition...period...end of conversation. If he can't get there by car, foot, or train, he simply ain't going. His aviatophobia (fear of flying) temporary morgueaphobia (fear of winding up under a sheet in a gymnasium) and Iraqnaphpobia (fear of being hijacked by Muslims and flying into a tall building) are putting a severe crimp in my own personal "bucket list" (things I want to do before I kick the bucket). My argument is that when it's our time to go, God will take us no matter where we are or what we are doing. His rebuttal is that Jesus said, "Lo, I am with you always." To him that says if you are stupid enough to get on a metal object larger than a Greyhound bus and expect it to get off the ground and stay there, you are on your own.

Flying is a great source of stress for me also, but I do it as a means to a happy end. My adrenal glands go into automatic over-drive the moment the pilot welcomes me aboard the flight, and they don't stop pumping adrenalin until the flight attendants remind everyone to check their belongings before departing the plane. Hangoveraphobia compels me to listen attentively to the sound of the pilot's voice for any signs of slurring, headache or nausea that might indicate he laid out in the airport lounge all night with a flight attendant. Emetobagaphobia (fear of vomiting into a paper bag) causes my stomach to lurch upward into my throat as the plane hurls down the runway. Once we are airborne, whirraphobia (fear of any change in the engine sound) causes my ears to become as keen as those of a blind person. Notimeforgoodbyeaphobia (fear the doors of the airplane will suddenly rip open and I will be sucked out at forty-thousand feet while strapped to a 200 pound metal object, my seat) causes me to grip the armrests so forcefully that my hands are paralyzed into claw formation when the flight is over. As the flight attendants demonstrate the obligatory "what to do in the unlikely event of a sudden loss of in cabin pressure" procedure, gimmedata-phobia (fear that my oxygen mask will work, but not the one belonging to the guy sitting next to me, and he will be Mike Tyson) causes me to hyperventilate. And what about the peace of mind you gain just knowing that you can use your seat cushion as a flotation device. Who do they think they are fooling? The last time I flew, it was out of Memphis on the way to New York. Other than the Mississippi River, the flight path to New York doesn't necessarily include any bodies of water large enough to accommodate a huge jetliner, which renders a flotation device as useless as a screen door on a submarine.

In the unhappy event of loss of cabin pressure, the flight attendants should be straightforward with the passengers and instruct them to, "Put your head between your knees and pray like crazy. If you are lucky, your eyes will pop out after loss of cabin pressure, and you will never know when the plane hits the water or ground and explodes into a giant fireball. We hope you enjoy your stay in eternity. Thank you for flyin' and dyin' with Delta."

However, if the worst does happen, you can take comfort in all the news headlines you will make when you go down in a blaze of glory in farmer McDonald's catfish pond in rural Georgia. All the news networks could broadcast the eyewitness account of how you met your fate.

"Hit wuz awful, jus awful. Me and my wife wuz sittin' on the porch watin' fer the mail to run. That's when we heered it. Sounded just like a freight train was comin' outta' the sky, but hit wuz a big jut areplane, Hit sounded like the end of the worl' when hit crashed nose first into my catfish pon. Hit kilt ever last one of my fish and all 'em people too. Pearl, my wife, is plum historical over this. I betche hit wuz zem terrists agin."

Tonight, when my husband comes home we are going to have a heart-to-heart discussion about this fear of flying dilemma. Wherever he wants to drive for our vacation is just fine with me. After writing this column, I realize I hate flying more than he does.

GRANDMA DELLA'S DUTCH OVEN

For several years I toyed with the idea of buying one. As a woman who was passed over by the love to cook gene, it was quite unusual that I often found myself browsing culinary shops captivated by lavishly displayed avant-garde cookware. It was always the ridiculously expensive Dutch ovens in trendy colors that pleaded, "Buy me! Look at me! I will make cooking fun and effortless, and you can be like them." By them, I am referring to my mother-in-law, Ouida Walters Rasberry and her mother Della Loper Walters, rolling pins down, two of the best cooks in Mississippi. Since Mississippi is the cradle of many of the best things about America--including down-home cooking, the Blues, country music, and rock and roll--that puts them in some pretty fair company.

Back in the spring, after exploring around his mother's shed and our adjoining land (his private Utopia), my husband burst through the back door and excitedly asked me to come outside because he had brought me a present. The key thing to understand is there is a huge disparity between the words brought and bought when used by my husband. Brought invariably means he found something that no one else in the world wanted, but in it he saw some redeeming quality that made it impossible for him to leave it behind. Over the last three decades he has "brought" me a plethora of basically unredeemable objects. For example, he thought I might like to decorate the mantle with a rusted out World War I helmet because it was an historic conversation piece. Once he presented me with a slop jar/chamber pot because you never know when you will require one. Just this summer, he hauled up a small mountain of sandstone rocks because they looked "old-timey."

With one hand placed daintily on his hip and the other one gracefully sweeping toward the prize, he struck an amusing resemblance to Vanna White. I thought he said, "Look what you've just won--grandma's cast iron Dutch oven!" As it was with the rocks, I have learned that you don't argue with a piece of Utopia. Instead of reprimanding him for his good intentions, I took the sad old pot into the kitchen and hoisted it into the sink with both arms. At first it didn't seem possible that I could salvage the neglected vessel that had surely been baptized in the hot fires of woodstoves then mysteriously banished to an old tractor shed. Most of the black iron on the outside had turned to rust, but the inside was still seasoned with the fat of countless homegrown meats. Then it hit me. If it could talk, it would tell of hard times during the Depression and down-home meals shared by innately happy folks. It would tell of days filled with more toil than rest, more laughter than tears, and more love than anything else. It would tell the story of my husband's people--my children's forbearers--and of a woman whose greatest joy in life was to cook for the ones she loved. After hours of scouring and an abundance of TLC, the orphaned pot that my husband brought me has become my prized possession.

It tips the scales at a whopping twelve pounds empty and when fully loaded with supper, it requires straining with both biceps to heave it into the oven. It still gives the food cooked in it a slight metal twang (not unlike the taste of an iron supplement) but with some salt and pepper you could slow bake an old pair of work boots to fork-tender palatability. Much like a hunting rifle, it could be dangerous if mishandled, and after each use it must be cleaned gently and greased generously before putting it away.

This Thanksgiving it will definitely play a major part in the cooking of our traditional dinner. Since I am next in line to become the matriarch, my home has now become the location of the Rasberry Thanksgiving dinner. All who will enter my house on Thursday are descendants of Grandma and Grandpa Walters either by marriage or blood. So many of the people we loved and learned from are no longer with us, but we will give thanks for the inimitably Southern customs and values they passed down to us and to those descendants who never had the privilege of laughing, giving thanks and feasting at their dinner table.

She was the standard bearer for grandmothers, and I can still hear her laughter and see her standing over the stove, silver hair twisted into a bun, content in her soul because she knew the true recipe for happiness. Grandma Della also left a mighty big pot to fill as far as Southern cooking goes. With a lot more practice and a little help from her Dutch oven, I think I can make her proud.

ANATOMY OF DIVORCE

Around Thanksgiving, the ReView ran my column, "Grandma Della's Dutch Oven." Reading that column is actually a pre-requisite for this column. If it were listed in a college catalog, it might be named "Unredeemable Objects Appreciation 101" taught by professor in residence Phillip Rasberry, D.P.T., M.S., M.T.C., and most notably— M.J.C. (Master Junk Collector). That being the case, this sequential column is aptly titled "Anatomy of Divorce"-- a dissection of the consequences of Unredeemable Objects Appreciation 101.

Just in case you didn't read the pre-requisite, here is a brief overview of the material covered: The course is the study of a well-educated, highly intelligent male member of the middle socio-economic class. Either by nurture or nature this individual suffers from a rare compulsion to bring unredeemable objects (worthless pieces of junk) home.

This time, my husband brought me the wrong object at the absolutely worst time. I certainly don't want this situation to escalate to the point where I am forced to appear before a judge to testify as to why I am seeking a divorce. If something doesn't give soon, this is most assuredly what the judge will hear: "Your Honor...it was the week before Christmas, and all through the house, pots and pans were ringing as my husband lounged on the couch...when out on the driveway arose such a clatter, I sprang from the stove to see what was the matter. When, what to my wondering eyes should appear, but a giant diesel truck, with Joe the driver, and Brian his sidekick, pulling a trailer so long, I knew in a moment it wasn't St. Nick. More rapid than eagles they came to the door, whistled and shouted, is Dr. Phil there? A wink in Joe's eye and a twist of his head, soon gave me to know I had something to dread. They spoke not a word, but went straight to their work, they unloaded the trailer, then turned with a smirk. Into the carport!! To the back of the wall!! Now dash away!! Dash away!! Dash away all!! After tripping and falling over the garden hose, upon giving a nod down the driveway they drove..."

"Please, Mrs. Rasberry, stop your rhyming. Christmas was weeks ago," the judge will warn.

"Sorry, your majesty. I had asked my husband for a new watch for Christmas. Granted, it cost slightly more than a Timex, but seeing it on Maria Sharipova's wrist in "Tennis" magazine filled me covetousness. At least I didn't ask for a Rolex."

"Mrs. Rasberry," the judge will scold, "Not getting the gift you wanted is a pitiful excuse for divorce. It's apparent to me that you are a selfish individual. I'm sure whatever he bought you was nice."

To the judge I will weep, "Sir, he didn't buy me anything. He had some guys from our church renovation committee bring me a seventeen-foot long, forty-year-old church pew. If that weren't bad enough, the cushion on it is the color of spicy-brown mustard. It's too long to put in the house, so it is sitting in the middle of the carport where I once parked my car." At this point, the judge will begin to listen with a sympathetic ear.

"My husband is an uncommonly decent person and the hardest working man I know, but this is the culmination of thirty years of his bringing me completely unredeemable objects. Also, your highness, the night they delivered it, I had just burned a pie in the oven. At my age, I am in a delicate state hormonally. What happened next was jarringly similar to that scene in *Christmas Vacation* when Clark Griswald didn't receive his usual Christmas bonus, but got a jelly of the month membership instead. Directly I called Joe, the deacon elf that delivered the pew, and told him to bring me every danged pew he could find and line them up on our carport. He's also a carpenter, so I asked him to construct a small steeple and place it on the gable of the carport. Also, if he knew of any bathtubs nobody was using, I asked him to bring one of those too. I informed him my husband planned to form a new church right there in the carport and call it the "For the Love of God Church of the Early Morning Risers and Junk Collectors." I told him services featuring guest speakers would be held every morning at 5:00 a.m., with free coffee, honey-buns and bathtub baptisms every Friday as needed — weather permitting. Your honor, this all sounds terribly sacrilegious, and I have asked for forgiveness. It's safe to say that the pew, my hormones and the devil made me do it."

With his hands pulling at his hair, the judge will then render his impartial decision. "I hereby declare this marriage dissolved on the grounds of unredeemable objects. Mr. Rasberry gets all the pews and the rest of the junk acquired during the marriage. Mrs. Rasberry, you get ½ of any remaining assets. Go buy yourself a watch and some Prozac."

As an aside, ya'll know I'm just kidding. He bought me the watch for Christmas after all. I gave him a big kiss and told him the pew could stay.

THE FAMILY JUNK WAR

After "Anatomy of Divorce" appeared in *The ReView* a couple of weeks ago, my husband swiftly retaliated by shifting his junk-collecting mode into overdrive. It appears that the word divorce written in bold ink in our weekly paper captured as much attention as the split of Brad and Angelina would on the cover of *People*. The Wellness Center was abuzz with members and physicians dropping by and calling his office wanting to know all about the new church as well as offering the names of reputable divorce attorneys.

The Honorable Pat Lightsey, mayor of Sandersville, former

beloved coach and feared algebra teacher, even dropped by to offer his condolences on our impending divorce. He thought it was tragic that an epic romance that began in high school, was coming to such a sorry end. He taught both of us algebra and geometry at Northeast Jones back in the early seventies. Let me clarify that statement. He taught Phil algebra and geometry while I simply occupied a desk in his classroom and stared vacantly at the algorithms he scribbled on the blackboard. Later, I found out that I wasn't stupid, but that the left side of my brain, which allows a person to think analytically, was underdeveloped.

The mayor is pleasantly surprised that the right side of my brain was able to absorb a little about the English language seeing as how I couldn't cipher an algebra equation if you held a gun to the left side of my head. If not for his patience and kindness, I would be the oldest sitting high school cheerleader in America--a living example of the mathematical concept of infinity (the length of time it would take for me to understand algebra), incapable of grasping the effect of negative and positive numbers in equations.

Coach, you will be proud to know that I have never forgotten the most critical mathematical constant — *pi R square*. I have just one burning question that has haunted me for years. If pie is square, then why are pie pans always round?

Let's get back to the original subject. In addition to an inability to cypher numbers, right-brained people have a tendency to serpentine the subject matter. My husband hasn't told me outright, but he has launched a covert operation to ramp up his junk collecting as payback for all the grief he has received through my columns.

He has dealt a low blow by recruiting help from our daughter and her fiancé. Erin, the right-brained fruit of my womb, who shares my algebraic handicap, has turned her back on me and joined the junky side. By her side is Big Ben Napier, a man whose Covington County family tree is cluttered (literally) with junk hoarders. With the engagement, my husband has definitely found the perfect protégé in his future son-in-law. Each of the three of them brings a special forte to the battle. My husband has motive and opportunity. My daughter, the traitor, has creativity and vision. My future son-in-law has the brawn, a rich gene pool and the steadfast desire to please his future wife and father-in-law. So far, our son has stayed neutral in the battle, but I fear that he will also turn to the dark side of the force and become the Darth Vader of the ongoing junk wars. Together, they hold the power to put this neat freak in the nervous hospital. Currently, an eighteen-year-old truck, pregnant with a new breed of old junk, is parked backward in my carport, guarding the infamous pew. Basically, I have lost all control over my once-tidy household. The scene is a hybrid of what would happen if the Beverly Hillbillies graduated from Ole Miss then joined forces with Sanford and Son and armed themselves with paint swatches, Pottery Barn catalogs and back issues of *Cottage Living* magazine.

A very wise man said that the pen is mightier than the sword. This pen is poised and ready to do battle against the newly formed Junk Brigade. WARNING! The more junk you drag up, the more rapidly the keys on my Mac will click and clatter. Just say no to junk, and I'll gladly put my sword away.

LIFE AT LITTLE MONTICELLO

Last summer when Phil and I took our pilgrimage to Gettysburg, we also took a fateful detour to Thomas Jefferson's Monticello in Charlottesville, Virginia. Monticello and the accomplishments of the author of The Declaration of Independence so profoundly impressed my husband that he has vowed to pattern the remainder of his life after the great Mr. Jefferson.

Looking back, I now realize that the turn my life has taken is more of my own doing than my husband's. It was totally my idea to visit Monticello as he had his mind set on the gods and generals of the Civil War, not Revolutionary era presidents. If only I had not set foot in that Monticello gift shop and let the tempting wares of history draw me in. Maybe it was the altitude or a simple case of vacation intoxication, but my conscience wouldn't let me leave there empty-handed. In hindsight, I honestly believe that Martha Stewart envy made me do it. As the clerk swiped my debit card, I thought smugly, "Take that Martha! You aren't the only woman in the world who is handy-dandy. I will be too. Ha!"

In our hotel that night I showed Phil my secret purchases, "Look what I bought at Monticello! Authentic seeds from Thomas Jefferson's garden!" His reaction? He couldn't have been happier if I had presented him with a bologna sandwich, cane pole and a box of crickets.

Jefferson designed and began construction of Monticello in 1768 on the summit of an 850-foot-high peak amidst 2,000 acres he inherited from his planter father. Of course, Jefferson was the third president of the United States, governor of Virginia, secretary of state, a philosopher, master gardener, architect, lawyer, and at the age of 76, was the founder of the University of Virginia. As president, he purchased the Louisiana Territory and launched the Lewis and Clark expedition. His second book collection became the nucleus of the Library of Congress. Ironically, he died on July 4, 1826---the 50th anniversary of the signing of the Declaration of Independence.

Exactly how does a man whose calling in life is admirable but not quite as illustrious as Mr. Jefferson's, who owns a parcel of in-fertile dirt in rural Mississippi and whose greatest architectural feat is building a bird house that resembles a missile, emulate the life of one of the most brilliant men in American history? For an optimistic man who sometimes borders on delusional, it's actually very simple.

He has convinced himself that twenty-five acres is par with two thousand. Instead of supervising the workers (there are no workers except for me) on horseback, he uses a tractor and bush-hog to mow down every dead or living thing in his path to forge a maze of trails that makes twenty-five acres truly seem like thousands. Rather than build a place of quiet reflection such as a garden pavilion, he admires his butterbeans from the comfort of a folding chair while reading Shelby Foote. Instead of tending a vineyard, he cultivates enough fig and blueberry trees to keep Nabisco in Fig Newtons and Smucker's in jam through a seven-year drought. When asked by his history-challenged daughter which side won at Gettysburg, he launches into a monologue that rivals Mr. Jefferson's presentation to the second Continental Congress.

Each day, life at Little Monticello begins and ends the same. As was Jefferson's habit, my husband rises before the sun and takes note of the weather. Jefferson kept a diary of weather patterns from his own observations and instruments. At Little Monticello, we tune into the Weather Channel. Before he leaves for work, he surveys the grounds and his postage stamp-sized garden terrace for crops that might need tending in the evening. So far, it has yielded 3 bell peppers, 4 Better Boy tomatoes, 6 hot (as Hades) peppers, one snake, a handful of speckled butterbeans and a baseball cap full of mutant, yard-long string beans. However, the squash crop has been bountiful with some of them growing to the size of clubs overnight. One morning they are the size of a peanut, and the next they are lethal weapons.

As it turns out, the *Pomme d'Amour* tomato seeds I purchased in the gift shop are related to the love plant, which was noted in the Bible for its reputed aphrodisiac qualities. It's no mystery now why ole' T.J. was the father of more than our Declaration of Independence. So far, it appears that the *lavandula angustifolia* and *lychnis chalcedonica* seeds that promised lavender flowers, fragrant leaves and bright scarlet blooms are nothing but common kudzu. If they come on like the squash did, our house will be completely engulfed by August.

Life at Little Monticello is tougher than we thought. It ain't easy being Martha Stewart and Thomas Jefferson. There is always next year.

MY CIVIL WAR WITH
BISCUITS, GREENS, & CHITTERLINGS

The last time I wrote a column featuring my husband, it was summer and we were living the good life at Little Monticello. Now that the seasons have changed, and his very bountiful crop of squash and tomatoes has been laid by, he has turned his attention to the winter crop and the tactics of Stonewall Jackson.

In the spirit of my foremothers, I even took special care to save some of the famous "love" tomato seeds for planting next spring. As more proof that I am not completely worthless in the kitchen, fig preserves made by these very hands are in the pantry waiting for someone to whip up a pan of homemade buttermilk biscuits for sopping. One of his patients also gave him a gallon of mayhaws that he, himself personally used to make jelly while I was off somewhere "losing a crop" by playing the worthless game of tennis. I do declare, he reminded me of Jonas Salk showing off a vial of his polio vaccine, when he held the jar up to the light and asked if I had ever seen anything more beautiful than that ruby-red jelly. It will cause much disquiet, but my preserves and his precious jelly will join a pan of homemade biscuits about the same time you see me join a quilting bee or make lye soap over a fire in the backyard.

My biscuits are more of the whop 'em variety that Yazoo City's Jerry Clower made famous in his down-home comedy act. Jerry quipped that it sounded like a young war had broken out in his neighborhood on Sunday mornings with all those whop 'em biscuits being laid open on countertops. He lamented that it was an abomination for southern women to commit such treason against their mothers and grandmothers. Of course, my husband agrees.

Early in our marriage, I tried several times to replicate the biscuits baked up at the hands of his loving mother. Even though I used the prescribed ingredients and kneaded them tenderly, they always came out of the oven completely unrecognizable. When I tearfully pitched them into the yard, they made a grave clunking sound and rolled across the driveway for a good twenty yards. Ole Champ, the prized birddog that Phil loved so much that he had his portrait painted on canvas, suspiciously pointed at them and then gobbled them down whole before he realized what he had ingested. God rest his soul.

All that remains of summer's crop is the skeleton of a lone okra stalk that reaches to the sky, replaced by a patch of the three greens that my husband believes is the key to longevity--turnips, mustard and onions. And, in the freezer lies the antithesis to longevity—30 pounds of pork chitterlings. Together, they are the bane of my existence and the proverbial thorn in the side of this woman who is quite happy living in the 21st Century.

The truth is my husband was born one hundred years too late. Although I do not believe in reincarnation, I believe he has some sort of spiritual attachment to the 1860's. Nothing else can explain his obsession with the Civil War, "old-timey" objects and doing things the primitive way as if electricity had never been invented.

Before he left for work in the winter storm warning last Thursday, his goodbye made me bristle like a cat, "It feels like chittlin' and turnip weather to me." The inflection in his voice and that look of a hungry Confederate general in his eyes led me to believe that a surprise attack was in the works. I had to steel myself for battle.

Toward dusk, when he didn't answer his cell phone, I knew the attack was imminent. I called my son's cell, and he answered straightway with that mischievous chuckle he does when he is and his father are on the offensive. "Hey Mom! Dad and I want to cook chittlins' tonight since my wife's out of town. You wouldn't want me to starve. We've got it under control if you can just help me make the cornbread, pick some turnips and green onions and maybe make a pitcher of tea, we will do the rest. You know we will cook the chittlins' outside and leave the kitchen smelling like a rose. Come on mom, it will be great since it's freezing and Christmas is coming."

I replied festively, "Instead of cornbread, I'll make a pan of my famous homemade biscuits."

Wavering on his end, "That's O.K. On second thought, we will pick up a bucket of chicken and cook the chittlins' later."

It worked like a charm. I flanked them.

BOOKS – THE SOUL OF MY HOUSE

Most people hold the misconception that realtors have a happy job where they get to show beautiful houses to agreeable people and make huge, easy commissions while having the time of their lives. All I'm going to say about that is that realtors work extremely hard for every penny they earn. Here is just one example: At the behest of a title insurance company, I found myself in a rather large cemetery searching for the grave of a man who died before I was born. The few remaining people who knew him told me that he was indeed deceased and had been in that condition for a long time. It was up to me, the diligent realtor, to prove it, and then locate and sweet talk two disinterested parties into swearing to it upon their lives in the presence of a notary. Incidentally, I had two hours before the closing to make it happen. Wandering through cemeteries looking for dead men isn't my idea of fun and only slightly assuaged by the compensation. That is why the knowledge that a good book is awaiting me at the end of a long day makes that day happier. After stumbling over tombstones, I couldn't wait to escape to my bedroom sanctuary to read. At last, I reached for my solitude. Panic set in when I realized that I had finished *The Girls*, a fascinating, far-from-uplifting novel about the oldest living conjoined twins, the night before. In my desperation, I jumped out of bed to scavenge through a wicker basket in my bedroom for something to read.

It held more than a dozen dusty paperbacks, the pages dogeared, ruffled and yellowing from multiple readings. Certainly there would be at least one suitable for an emergency situation such as this. Strange bedfellows rested together in the basket.

"Oh, here's *The Guardian* by Nicholas Sparks...a decent book, but not compelling enough for a re-read. *To Tame a Rebel*... romantic swill masquerading as history, but I drank up every passionate, breathless word of it. This one has potential...Danielle Steele's *Miracle*. What was that one about? Not that it matters. Her books are all so predictable—girl or boy loses love, finds it again, gets pregnant or impregnates, perfect baby is born, lives nauseatingly happily ever after (just fill in the blanks) in a _____ by the_____. Here's *Johnny Cash*. It's new to the basket since I read it last fall. He fell into a ring of fire and walked the line for June Carter. *Uncle Tom's Cabin*...how poignant to find it lying beside *The Killer An-*

gels—one a catalyst for the other. Abraham Lincoln said Harriet Beecher Stowe was the little lady who caused a big war. *The Killer Angels* depicted the beginning of the end of that big war at Gettysburg. No luck tonight, I need peace and quiet, not war.

Sadly, I didn't love books as a child. There were simply too many other exciting, outdoor diversions. In high school, assigned book reading was the scourge of those otherwise free and easy years. It's something I'm not proud of, but this upstanding student fudged on book reports by gleaning the high spots. The only person I cheated was myself. It wasn't until college that it dawned on me that skillful writers must be ravenous readers.

I'm not certain when my love affair with books began. It wasn't a love-at-first-book moment, but bloomed gradually over the years. Margaret Mitchell's *Gone With the Wind* might have been the one that blew a tiny spark into a flame. After watching the 1977 mini-series, my sister convinced me to read *The Thornbirds* because she claimed the book was so much better than the television version. Australia, Father Ralph de Bricassart and the notion that reading could take me anywhere and with anyone I chose to go captivated me.

My fingers have eagerly turned thousand of pages this past year alone and possibly millions since my love affair began. Every room in my house, from the kitchen to the laundry room, contains books. A house without books is like a body without a soul. A nightstand without one or several is an abomination. Since becoming enamored with books, I've never known any heartache that an hour's worth of reading didn't soothe. When I step into a bookstore, I cannot understand why I should ever have to leave. Every truth, beauty, wisdom, belief, inspiration, and every fantasy can be found between the covers of a book.

As the years take their toll on my body, I hope that my eyes can still perceive and my mind can still absorb words in books. They say you can't judge a book by its cover; but I believe that you can judge a reader by his books. It would be a little embarrassing to die in the middle of some quasi porn such as *To Tame a Rebel*. As a precautionary measure, Homer's *The Odyssey* will have a permanent home on my nightstand.

THE OLD COWBOY BOOTS

It's funny how inspiration for a column finds me when I've given up looking for it. A few evenings ago my column literally came clomping through the back door on my daughter's feet. Married life agrees with her and she has never been happier; but she still likes to recharge her batteries at our house — her once and forever home.

Shoes have now become a recurring theme in my columns, but when I saw the old cowboy boots sitting on the hearth in the glow of the fireplace, I immediately knew I had to tell their story. It appeared that Erin had levitated out of them, leaving the toes pointed slightly outward, and was transported to an oversized chair where she was nestled and sleeping like a baby.

The original owner of the boots was finishing up some paperwork, a decades-long, nightly ritual that I both loathe and appreciate. In a peculiar sort of way, the boots have become the mascot for a career that began thirty-four years ago.

When I look back through my wiser, much dimmer eyes, we were unbelievably naive newlyweds in 1975 during Phil's final year of physical therapy school. When he left to do a six-week internship in Abilene, Texas, I moved back home to my parents' house and went to work at Commercial National Bank. We were in the process of renovating an old house (our very first) when he left for Texas, so I poured myself into the project to ease the loneliness and the lovesickness. As it turns out, he was assuaging his by learning the Cotton-Eyed Joe and the Texas two-step in his brand new, elephant-hide cowboy boots.

From all accounts, Abilene is as Texas as Texas gets. It is a flat, dry, windblown, treeless land inhabited by larger-than-life characters, cattle and rattlesnakes. And, everybody—from newborns to maw-maws--wears cowboy boots.

In a land full of larger than life characters, the legend of Bill Snowden has been elevated to Bigfoot proportions at our house. Standing nearly seven feet with his boots and Stetson hat, the director of West Texas Rehab Center cast a long shadow upon the "therapy boys" from Mississippi. His first assignment was for them to skedaddle on over to the Tradin' Post and buy themselves a pair of cowboy boots and a western shirt. He couldn't abide his interns looking like greenhorns in their loafers and button-down collars. Don't waste your money on just any kind of boots he advised, "Soles may come and soles may go, but elephant hide will last a lifetime." His second assignment was for them to meet him that night at the

Tumbleweed Inn for baptism in Ernest Tubb music and two-steppin'
lessons with his lovely wife.

In his haste and trying to save money that he didn't have in
the first place, my husband bought a pair of Dan Post, elephant hide
boots on sale for what would be about three hundred in today's dollars. The only problems were that they were two sizes too small and
a color I would describe as burnt orange manure. When he returned
from Texas, I strongly suggested that the fashion disasters be retired
to a closet where they sat aging like fine wine for the next thirty-one
years.

Fast forward to the winter of 2006. Cowboy boots suddenly became haute couture on college campuses and the older and
more broken down, the better. After being banished from society,
the boots suddenly became very chic and the object of every coed's
desire. Burnt orange manure evolved into the hottest new color—
cognac, and matched Erin's BCBG bag splendidly. They never again
glided across the sawdust of a Texas dance hall floor. However, they
did score a touchdown in Vaught-Hemingway Stadium one midnight and explored the length and breadth of the Grove and The
Square a hundred times. So what if she has to wear three pair of
socks to keep them on her feet. Since you now have to wait for an
elephant to die of natural causes to harvest its hide, Erin finally possessed something that couldn't be purchased anywhere at any price
— almost unheard of on the campus of Ole Miss.

Despite all our good intentions, Phil never took me to
Abilene and I never met the tall drink of water who taught him
much of what he knows about physical therapy and the entirety of

what he knows about Texas, dayncin', rattlesnake roundups and, of course, boots. The only picture I have of him is in my mind.

Just as Bill Snowden predicted, soles and souls have come and gone, and even our first house was torn down, but that old pair of boots has remained a constant in a world where most things are fleeting. Call me sentimental and sappy, but I find something very comforting in that.

A TALE OF TWO SISTERS

Buster came into our world seven years ago— the same week that my father-in-law left it. He was a confounding mixture of coonhound, bird dog and cattle herder. His bark was so deep and ominous, the sound of it resembled a foghorn in the night, warning ships to stay away from the rocks. In order to understand the significance of his arrival, you need to hear the whole story.

James Rasberry, the patriarch of our family and a friend to many throughout the county because of his political career during the sixties, seventies and early eighties, had just lost his battle with Lou Gehrig's disease. In the style of Edward Bloom, the unforgettable character in the movie *Big Fish*, he was a teller of tall tales who freely gave advice whether you asked for it or not. The amazing thing is, politicians and constituents of his era relished hearing his tall tales, sought his advice, and gravitated toward his charismatic personality.

I believe God performed a small miracle when Buster ambled into my mother-in-law's yard the day of the funeral. Don't misunderstand, because I don't believe in re-incarnation or ghosts, but that dog sure did remind us for the world of Papaw. Call me crazy, but I do believe that my father-in-law, a newcomer in Heaven, gave God some unsolicited advice. "You can do what you want to, but since I'm up here, and she's down there alone, Weeder needs somebody to take care of her. I'm just telling you."

Not long after Buster settled into his divinely appointed position as watchdog and booger chaser, a handsome, white female of the boxer persuasion wandered up to my mother-in-law's back door. For Buster and Betty, it was love at first sight. As you might guess, it didn't take long for nature to take its course. Shortly after their eight pups were born, Betty mysteriously disappeared. My mother-in-law became their surrogate mother until we found a good home for all but two of them. She kept the spotted pick of the litter and named her Susie. We adopted the solid white runt and cleverly named her Lilly.

I have always been skeptical of amazing stories where animals save their owner's lives or travel hundreds of perilous miles to find their way home. I thought they were simply creatures that didn't possess reasoning abilities, or the heart and soul of human beings.

Susie and Lilly turned this skeptic into a full-fledged believer.

From the beginning, I could tell they knew they were sisters. For several years, every morning, as sure as the sun rose, Susie would trot through the woods to visit with Lilly at my house. Outside the kitchen window, on a small rise beneath the pines, I would watch them with amusement as they interacted. They would sit there motionless, cheek-to-cheek, for several minutes, as if they were telling sisterly secrets to one another. By the time I left for work, Susie had headed back home to check on her mistress.

Three years ago, Buster was shot by a disgruntled neighbor for attempted cattle herding. Shortly afterwards, Lilly followed my husband down the road in a rainstorm and was struck by a passing car. The whole family mourned the loss of Buster and Lilly, but it was Susie that grieved the most. It was heartbreaking to look out my window every morning and see the poor thing sitting there day after day, waiting for her sister to return.

Since Buster's demise, Susie has been my mother-in-law's sole companion and watchdog. She follows her to the garden and accompanies her on walks. The two of them together are a beautiful sight. Every Friday at precisely 10:00 A.M., Miz Ouida takes her weekly 1/2 mile drive to Jenny Myrick's beauty shop. Susie always escorts her there and naps in the sun until Miz Ouida emerges with a fresh hairdo.

Three weeks ago, Miz Ouida suffered a stroke. Since the morning we took her to the hospital, Susie has kept a vigil in the yard waiting for us to bring her best friend home. Jenny called me to check on one of her favorite, darling lil' ole ladies. During our conversation, she told me a truly amazing story about Susie. For the past three Fridays, at exactly 10:00 A.M., Susie has shown up at her beauty shop. Last Friday, Jenny was shocked to see a sad-faced Susie on her hind legs, paws on the beauty shop window, peering through the glass, hoping to find Miz Ouida.

We can only speculate as to what makes animals perform heroic feats and behave with such human-like characteristics. Personally, I believe that dogs in particular instinctively recognize love when they receive it. They return it in the only way they can with undying loyalty, a wagging tail and weekly visits to a beauty shop if necessary.

THE PINK PONTIAC

My husband's father gave it to the family as a Christmas present in 1963. It was a 4-door sedan constructed of solid steel and chrome with 389 cubic inches under the hood, 17 feet 8 inches from bow to stern and more horsepower than a family of four could ever use. Gas was cheap, and the bigger and the brawnier the car, the better. James Rasberry was a product of the Depression and a member of the generation that brought this country through World War II. For those reasons and others that are more complicated, men of that generation had a life-long love affair with new cars.

I wasn't there that day when my future father-in-law wore down the eager car salesman, but the image of it is as clear to me as tinkling Christmas bells. The showroom smells like new rubber, fresh paint and faux leather, aphrodisiacs for those stricken with new car lust. Barely ten years old, a chubby little boy sits in the waiting area, legs fidgeting, fingers crossed, about to burst with excitement at the prospect of riding home that Christmas Eve in a brand new "wide track" Pontiac. He sat behind the massive steering wheel, but couldn't quite see over the dash, then stretched out on the back seat and dreamed of all the places he could go if only his daddy would drive it home.

The salesman, anxious to be home with his family, threw in the towel. He offered his right hand in defeat, "Mr. Rasberry, you've got yourself a deal." Final price--$3344.04--plus the trade-in on a 1959 Catalina.

1964 was a good year for my future family as it was for my house on the other side of the county. They bought an 8 mm home movie camera, hit the road and wore the new right off the Catalina. Filmed in exotic locations such as the Suwannee River and the Memphis zoo, the movies play a quarter note faster than real life as the ten-year-old dreamer and his little brother strum imaginary guitars, dance and ham it up for the camera.

For the next several years, the car is easel for the canvas that portrays their family life. In each successive picture, the chubby boy grows taller and leaner until one day there is a picture of him behind the steering wheel, ready to take control of the untapped power under the hood. This is where I come into the picture.

My heart skipped a beat when I heard the low groan of the engine coming up the driveway. For my very first date, I applied too much eyeliner, failed at straightening my hair and bathed myself in Ambush perfume. A confident young jock wearing sideburns, tight Levis and a letterman's jacket stepped out of the carriage that was about to whisk me away to adolescent freedom. I slid a quarter mile across the seat to his side before he put the car in drive. The smell of Brut and Ambush filled the car as we zoomed down the road, free at last from the bondage of childhood.

During his high school years, the Catalina served as the unofficial mascot of the football team—their symbol of independence, roomy enough to accommodate half the team and powerful enough to hang with the sportier muscle cars. By then, the original cranberry red paint had faded to a deep pinkish color. Since boys will be boys, they christened her with a slightly naughty name that refers to the female bosom. We now exclusively call her by that name, but never in the company of strangers.

The old girl was finally handed down to the younger brother Danny, who went on to make his own memories with her. After that, her life as a primary source of transportation was over, so they mothballed her in the shed where she became a shelter for transient yard dogs and stray cats.

In 1992, after twenty-nine Christmases and a million miles of memories, my father-in-law was ready to let her go if my husband could revive her. At first I resented the money he spent to get her on her feet again and secretly wished that his daddy had purchased a muscular Mustang instead of a 4-door femme fatale.

My resentment (or possibly jealousy) of her has now subsided, and our children think it is super cool to have such a grand dame to cruise around in. Getting her primed and cranked requires much coaxing, and more often than not, she just says no. In the past, she responded only to my husband's touch, but has recently taken a liking to younger men. She coughs and chokes, trembles and blows smoke, but once you get her fired up, she's the queen of the road, soliciting stares and finger pointing when we glide down the road astride her wide hips.

Mostly now, we take her out on holidays or when we feel the need to be young and frisky again. The most common reaction from love-struck onlookers is, "Would you sell her?"

"Nope, not for a million dollars." In her heart, she holds many secrets and the memories of forty-four Christmases. She is a gift that just keeps on giving.

photo by McAlister Creative

KAREN CLARK RASBERRY is a life-long resident of Jones County and Laurel, Mississippi. She is a nationally published writer and currently writes a weekly column for *The ReView*. She has been married for 35 years and has a grown son and daughter. This is her second book.

Made in the USA
Monee, IL
25 April 2021

66844085R00132